# THE BOOK OF INTENTION

## Stephen Ridley

**BALBOA.**
PRESS

A DIVISION OF HAY HOUSE

ISBN: 978-1-4525-6229-2 (sc)
ISBN: 978-1-4525-6230-8 (e)
ISBN: 978-1-4525-6231-5 (hc)
Library of Congress Control Number: 2012920703

Balboa Press books may be ordered through booksellers or by contacting:
Balboa Press
A Division of Hay House
1663 Liberty Drive
Bloomington, IN 47403
www.balboapress.com
1-(877) 407-4847

Printed in the United States of America
Balboa Press rev. date: 11/26/12

*For my Father, both of them.*

# THE BOOK OF INTENTION

*It is only with the heart that one can see rightly.*
*What is essential is invisible to the eye.*
*- Antoine de Saint-Exupery*

*__Those who would control are__*
*__not open to question.__*

# 1. INTRODUCTION

WHEN I WAS A YOUNG boy I often wondered if I was meant to be here. I felt like an alien; I couldn't have been more than six years old.

I have wondered since then if those thoughts were linking me to the past, or to the future. The truth is that they were linking me to both. But more importantly it was the start of the journey, one that I had made many times before, to reconnect with all in the temporal world and then reconnect that back to where we came from, and even more importantly to help others to do so. We are all capable of that, therefore my journey is also, in some small way, the same as yours. That reconnection is our story, one that I will try to tell through the story of my own journey.

It raises searching questions and uses analogies wherever possible, as I have come to learn to use these to help explain reality through the journey of my own thoughts, connecting them through the process of reflection, major learning experiences and the knowledge that has been acquired and developed.

Much as I felt at the age of six, some of these concepts and this learning might seem alien to you at first. Please stop to pause, and reflect. Most of us have ears that can hear, and eyes that can see. We know they exist, and yet we have never 'seen' them directly.

You might say to yourself, 'but I have seen them in a mirror and on others and I know I am the same as them!'. Once you have reflected on this for a while, you will be ready to start the journey based on reflections of yourself and observation of others who are just like you, a path to understanding, knowledge and enlightenment, connecting across all faiths and belief systems.

When this happens, most will be able to truly see others and hear others, and then all will be ready to touch the lives of others for the common good. In that way, the transformation of consciousness that reconnects everything will manifest good intentions for every Human Being and every other Being.

The One Project, of which this is a part, is about the Universe. It intends a better world for all Human Beings based on love.

*The Book of Intention* expands upon *The Book of Life*, explaining the nature of reality, why we are here, and how to grow to a higher level of consciousness, towards a higher self, both as practical Human Beings and through the spirituality and connection that is innate within everyone.

This work is both a channelled and experiential understanding of holistic philosophy, psychology, healing and prophecy, uniting the work of the avatars and their messages, a Book of *knowledge*. It is about learning, healing and teaching, intending to unite all Human Beings as One.

If *The Book of Life* is analogous to *the Tree of Life*, *The Book of Intention* is how to nurture the tree that grows within each of us, pointing the way to the sustainability of Human Beings on Earth, and our reconnection with the Source of Creation, the transformation of human consciousness.

*God is the good in all.*

# 2. DOES GOD EXIST?

Do I believe in God?

No, I do not believe in God, but I *know* that God exists. I have both surrender and faith.

*Knowledge* is not the same as a belief, an opinion or simply 'blind' faith. How true knowledge is attained is described in Chapter 8 - the number is based upon the symbol for infinity connecting Heaven and Earth.

However, let's say for the moment that you do not believe in God, or that you are uncertain of God's existence. This might be for a variety of reasons, especially if this is based on what life has taught you so far and the pain that you have felt.

Now, let's say that God would be your concept of the ideal. Most people are essentially capable of understanding this. Then, if you do have that concept, God *must* exist as a thought of the ideal *within you*.

That thought would probably make God smile.

The English word for God is derived from the German word '*Gott*'. This in turn is derived from the German word '*gut*', meaning 'good'. God is the same as Allah, YHWH, Vishnu, Vahiguru, Ahuramazda, Serendipity, the Dao and The One, plus many other 'names' - that which Is; is meant to Be; is Being; is Creation; is the Source of Creation; is the Way; is the Universe, at all levels.

So, do you believe in *good*?

Using the logic of the words we use to describe something and the symbols that can be associated with these words (which are our main ways of communicating common concepts to each other), then God must also include our (or your) concept of the ideal or common good, even if at the moment you think that this ideal does not exist within this world.

If you thought that you were an atheist or agnostic, just knowing that you have a concept of the *common good* or an ideal is proof that you have just contradicted yourself about what you think you know about God or good! That is why opinion, which is based on assumptions or gaps in knowledge, can only ever give a partial knowledge of the true nature of reality and of all of creation that you *know* you a part of.

There are some who believe that Jesus was the spirit of God manifest, or the will of God, the Christ, manifest on Earth, but without really knowing why.

Jesus has many different names in different languages. The most common are transliterations of his real name. If you conjoin Isa (in Islam), Jesus and Joshua and try to come up with a common pronunciation, you will probably approximate to the pronunciation 'Yeeschwah'. People of other faiths will recognize this as 'YHWH', the previously *unpronounceable* name of God. This has commonly been pronounced since that time as Yahweh, or Jehovah, as Human Beings have no knowledge of how the original Aramaic name would have been pronounced or heard. The name was even alluded to in the motion picture '*Avatar*', along with the eternal message of overcoming your fears, connecting with everything and learning to *ride the shadow*.

Yet I also know that Jesus (or the name *Iesus* in Latin) was the name of a Human who was also a Being. He was an avatar that appeared many times, a *warrior of the Light*, fighting the forces of darkness since some of the angels, the higher and original creations, had fallen. He appeared many times before his time as Jesus and many times since. He was the same innate Being connected to Michael.

His Being, the Christ within, will appear again, but many will not know or understand. The reason is that it is the *message* that is important, since it came from the Source of Creation in many different forms, including the Buddha who taught about reincarnation and karma in order that Human Beings could *learn* what they needed to know from their many lives before being able to return to Source.

The basis of all true faith systems is eternal love, whether this is, for example, from Zoroastrianism, Judaism, Hinduism, Islam, Sikhism or *Christ*ianity. The primary thing to understand is that if the message is about love then it will always come from Source, because Source *is* love, and will always be because creation is an act of love. Creation and love will *always* be for the common good because true love is gentle and self-less. A God of love must therefore be a *gentle* God, because any other supposition would be a contradiction. Therefore all suppositions of another god are demons created within the mind.

Do we learn this or is this understanding innate within all of us? According to Sister Frances Dominica, founder of the first children's hospice in Oxford, England, 'Faith is caught, not taught', which leads to some poignant questions:

Is there intrinsically any real difference between the faiths of love? Did not the major religions and ideologies go to war in the name of God, each of them claiming that 'if God is on our side, who can be against us'?

Part of our minds allows this separation. There is no such thing as 'us', because 'us' is a relative term to force a temporary distinction with 'them' that creates an *artificial* separation between essentially the same thing, and that in itself is a contradiction. This is because love cannot be separated from creative existence and a focus on non-self, or is seeing something that we connect with in others that automatically negates a perceived divide between 'us'.

Since contradictions are a counter of two opposites, within reality they cannot be true since reality must *include* all things. You could argue that a distinction is a perception, and perceptions exist in reality, but even that is only a one-sided perception since there is another perception that contradicts that one! In other words, all distinctions are contradictions that essentially cancel each other out.

The reason that we use distinctions is to make sense of the physical or temporal world. These distinctions do not exist within the spiritual world, they are simply a duality. If you doubt this, quantum mechanics may provide a clue: observation of a particular particle will make the particle change its relative position, suggesting that we are looking at the same particle from the same particle!

Another way of looking at it is by comparing the size of two different objects of perceived different size. From the perspective of the smaller object the other is larger. From the perspective of the larger object the other is smaller. If one of them did not exist *in comparison* to the other, such a perception would not exist. Human Beings are a mirror and refection of completeness, a part of creation in His image.

Further clues are provided by Albert Einstein's theory of relativity, in other words that all perceptions are relative to each other. To help understand this, imagine for one moment that you are observing four planetary bodies, three lined-up vertically and the fourth to the right of the bottom-placed body. (You can try drawing this). Light energy will travel from the top to the bottom right planetary body by 'bending' around the body of the middle one, yet also travel directly from the top body to the bottom right. The *distance* is not the same, yet the light arrives at the same time. All observation of energy is therefore relative to the viewpoint and the interaction of other bodies. That is why scientists will never find a Grand Unifying Theory, because no such theory is able to exist other than by 'observing' the whole or the Universe as One, and that is not possible from a limited viewpoint. It is much like trying to measure the length of a needle from two points upon its' tip!

Relating this to Human Beings, we are a just a momentary 'blip' in the 'time' of creation and 'us' is therefore a semantic to distinguish the artificial *distance* between 'us' and 'them'. Yet, if we had not been born within the assumed group that we call 'us', we could have been born in one of the assumed groups we call 'them', and vice versa.

If we could switch between the two groups at will, we would see the perspective of both sides at the very same moment and see clearly that there is no truthful reality as 'us' and 'them'. In other words it is ultimately no more important being born into a Jewish family rather than a Hindu one, or taking up the vocation of 'nursing' as opposed 'being a doctor', both of whom are essential parts of the same family of medicine. Within medicine we have both men and women, yet this does not distinguish their profession, etc.

*Stephen Ridley*

So the point is this: we are *all* part of the family of creation, regardless of our age, gender, sexual orientation, physical ability, culture, race or religion, including other species and all other things that are created. Anything else is *judgment* of others, and that is neither a selfless gift nor is it our given place to do so. In addition, we become part of creation when *we create with all other things* that are created. God, even if only seen as the creative will of good, would demand that to be good we would have to think and act for the good *together*.

Human Beings are conscious and free will, as are the Beings and angels that preceded them and, through that evolutionary process, Human consciousness has become energy observing its own form, and able to *understand* what it is to be good. In other words, Human Beings are a form of energy that has developed consciousness of creation, including its' own. Was that created? Of course it was, by the energy of the Universe. Was there a beginning? Of course there wasn't - what could there have been before the beginning if not another beginning?

The Universal and therefore true question is not *'what is the meaning of life'*, but rather *'what is the purpose of life'*? Desire is a motivating force that gives meaning, and love is an intrinsic need and pursuit of all. However, it is creative direction that gives purpose. Aligning the two around love unites the physical, emotional and intellectual with the ideal. So, even if you do not believe in God's existence, the pursuit of the ideal has no less meaning for creation, otherwise everything is meaningless. This *creative* learning experiment we call Earth is One within an infinite of many. God bless Douglas Adams.

If God (or good) is creation or creative will, then God must also represent perfection, since the world must be the best of all possible worlds to date, otherwise a better world would exist.

8

However, we also know that a better world is possible because we have ideals of that better world. If we are a part of creation, and anything else must be a contradiction, then our ideal must be the ideal of creation and therefore also of God or good. The worst that anyone can therefore say of God is that He or She is our concept of the ideal.

If we look back to religion, distinctions between the major faiths and the Christ Being in particular, what would the Christ (God's manifestation and will) have thought of greed and corruption? More pragmatically, what would the Christ have thought of temples, churches, mosques and synagogues closing their doors that could be opened in times of trouble to protect, cloth, feed and house the homeless and destitute? Do you really think that praying for your own well-being is what the Christ would want before you have prayed for others? What would be said about war and conflict?

I looked for many years to find answers and the common ground between some of the major religions as a proxy for the truth, by trying to identify the overlap between the faiths of Hinduism, Buddhism, Judaism, Christianity and Islam, much like the overlapping areas of the five Olympic rings used in the symbol for the world's Olympic Games. There has been much written about each faith, yet most of it was *not* written by the respective avatars but by others after they had died. However, after many years I realized that I was looking at this the wrong way round and from a particular perspective, much like a paradox. In my experience, all life is a paradox.

If we move the rings apart and look at their *core message*, the point or the circumpunct at the centre of each of these faiths, the essential message is identifiable as similar, if not the same, within each of them. The centre is an essential part of the circumference of the circle; therefore the two cannot be distinguished as being separate from each other, much like the true or sustainable messages within all faith systems of the good.

Initially I considered Buddhism and Hinduism, the essence of the messages respectively being: 'connect Heaven and Earth through spirituality' and 'revere the essence in all objects'.

Then I thought that God thought…. *Not all Human Beings got that, perhaps it was too difficult for everyone, so how about you look after family and community? For that I will give you…* Judaism. But not everyone understood that either, perhaps because they thought their families were 'us' and others were 'them', rather than focusing on all loved ones, including all new people that they met and were able look after within the communities that they had created. 'Exclusive' communities cannot by definition include the wider whole.

So I think that God, probably initially exasperated but ever patient, thought…. *If you can't be inclusive within communities, no matter who is in them, how about you treat someone else as you would wish to be treated, one-to-one?* This was the main message of Jesus. Jesus had effectively borrowed 'The Golden Rule' from those who came before; essentially *love another as one-self.* Not everyone listened, including those who claimed to be *Christ*ians. The conflict continued.

Then came an additional core message from the Prophet Mohammed: *surrender your will (Islam) and live within community (Umar)*, lessons in building upon the previous teachings. The conflict continued.

The last main avatar after Mohammed was Nanak Dev who propounded that there are *good values* by which to live (Sikhism). Still the conflict continued.

These 'core' teachings are more or less chronological and have the same essential meaning. What surrounds and has been added to these messages is less important than the core of the messages which is in essence the same: it one of *love*.

Lao Tse, another ancient writer and this time a Chinese born avatar, also wrote the Tao Te Ching, the Book of the Way of Virtue (or Integrity). The teaching was to live in harmony with the Tao (or Way), which is the essence or the Source of everything that exists in nature.

We are all a part of nature, created from the same essence as the Universe, and therefore we are all from the same Source. These avatars talk of the same thing, being true to oneself and therefore to The One, or to Source. One *is* love. Love and virtue *is* the Way. Therefore *love* and *virtue* is the only Way that is sustainable for our reconnection with Source.

Zoroaster preceded these avatars with the message that there is one God or, put more simply, God *is* One. It is mostly this lack of understanding, knowledge and acceptance that creates the root cause of conflict and separation within Human Beings. If we want to live as One, then we must think and act as One, nurturing our diversity but with the same *shared values* that God would regard as being for the *common good*, or *for all creation*.

Once I had understood this, the way back to reconnection with the Source of Creation became increasingly obvious, the chronological reverse of the core messages: live by good values, surrender your will, love one another, build inclusive communities, revere *all* objects on Earth, and reconnect Heaven and Earth as One, a religious and spiritual *'quid pro quo'*.

The result is an end of war, conflict and sin. The word 'sin' derives from the Latin *'sine'* meaning *without*, in a religious, spiritual or moral context *without God* or the common good. In other words, without sin, it would be the end of separation from One *or* another within the *whole of creation* regardless of which faith system you were born into or you have chosen that best helps you to understand *Holiness*, which means the whole or One-ness.

To be *holistic* we must also learn to collectively focus on and change some of the words we use, since, to produce a positive intention and outcome, all words must be the words of good, or God, for all and One. This happens because our consciousness is developed based on our words and their relative meanings and distinctions. Words will influence our understanding and psyche within both the unconscious and conscious mind, which in turn influences our behaviours, forms our attitudes and results in our accepted cultures or ways of living and *Being*.

For example, when we take a holiday it was meant to be a Holy Day, or Whole Day, or a One Day, when we could reconnect with each other within our communities. Some have changed this to 'vacation' which is such an empty word! We have also started to use terms such as myself, meaning 'me' as separated from 'us', let alone 'them'. There have been many changes to language, some good and some not so good. The original and correct term is *one-self.*

The importance of words relates to having right thoughts, right actions and positive manifestations of our intentions, as language reinforces conscious behaviour and ultimately unconscious attitudes that result in semantics such as 'us' and 'them', and sin (or separation) from one-another, and therefore Source.

To illustrate the potential falsity of distinctions further, we might call a tree a tree. Most people would recognize a picture of one, and yet no two trees look the same, in other words they do not have *exactly* the same form as each other. They are essentially the same and yet unique. They also change individually over time; they grow and their energy is recycled. Trees are perfect fractals, like the snow-drops that fall from the sky, rooted in and an integral part of the Earth. Imagine a tree as part of the living Earth reaching for the Heavens, a symbol for the Tree of Life, another reason why they might be so important to Human Beings. Imagine also snow-drops as the Heavens watering the Earth, to sustain the cycle. Maybe you can now see the cycle and connection. Also, like frozen snow-drops, maybe we Human Beings must too melt our frozen hearts to help sustain the Earth, and free our minds to accept the intention and outcome of a collaborative, constructive and benevolent society and Way of Being that is fully in harmony with the environment that gives us life.

So why are trees, and snow-drops, not exactly the same as each other?

*Diversity creates life* and fills every niche, increasing the possibility of more interaction, learning, creation and growth. Charles Darwin explained this beautifully before a dark philosophy tried to change this to 'survival of the fittest'. If this latter, corrupted so-called 'philosophy' had been true, I am sure that if Human Beings had competed *against* each other rather than collaborated during the last Ice Age they would not have survived, and we would not have been able to talk about it right now!

In much the same way as trees and snow-drops, we are all unique but we have the most important creative features in common, including our innate and conscience-enabled acknowledgement or understanding of what would be regarded as either the common *good* or having the common concept of God as our ideal. *We are all a part of the whole* within the whole of creation, including trees, and the water and sun-light that sustains them, plus all other things which help to keep Human Beings alive. Anything else is non-sense, a massive contradiction.

I need to explain *critical mass as* an important concept in understanding the next paragraphs.

Imagine a children's playground see-saw. If the weight of one child on each end is heavier than that of the other, the see-saw will go down or up (depending on your perspective). If the children are the exactly the same weight as each other and do not exert their energy, the see-saw will remain stationary. Critical mass is therefore effectively the weight or energy that is transferred from one end to the other to create movement, balance and life in an object as a whole, in this case the *moving* see-saw and the children, and in this case for the joy of the children. The children can also interact using their own energy to create movement and create a new critical mass. This is the nature of change, where new but temporary systems of form, shape and movement are created.

Seemingly unalterable objects also have critical mass. They exist in form and content at different levels, for example, the laws of physics co-creating the laws of chemistry and then co-creating the laws of biology. However, they are inherently unstable if they configure to the extent that that they are in conflict with their environment which permitted their possibility to come into being in the first place.

In such cases, the environment or conditions outside the 'unalterable' object will change the configuration of the objects within its' realm to the extent that that the configuration is deconstructed, consequently to become re-usable within another possible state of affairs in a new or modified form. Examples of this include cultural change (such as the rise and fall of empires) and biological change (such as extinction of species, and the death of an individual).

But some forms have qualities that pertain to the truth, in that they pervade time. Such examples include fractals (within mathematics), observable patterns within physics, the aesthetics of physical form, and the harmony within music. This is the basis of *string theory*, where all things (objects) are connected and can exist because they are either in perfect balance with their environment or are an intrinsic value (property) of it, which are the same state of affairs from either an external or internal perspective.

Material objects are therefore critical mass *systems* sustained by ever changing energy, for example the Human body. New, expended and transferred energy creates movement and balance within the whole. The energy within a seemingly fixed object may change several times, but as long as the critical mass within the object or system is maintained, the object continues to exist. No matter how much the component energy changes, if critical mass of the object is not maintained, the object or system will cease to exist. Therefore critical mass is essential to the existence of any particular object or system, including the living body of a Human Being. The energy during life is simply *borrowed*. Remove or add a component of the system, including its' energy, and the behaviour of the system changes.

For example, the cells in a Human body, each one a critical mass system in its own right, are replaced throughout each lifetime.

Old age occurs when cell replacement cannot maintain a critical mass, the net replacement of worn out cells. Therefore all material objects that exist, and all movement and any change in the form or shape of any object, are supported by an underlying change in the energy that they use.

Change that is at a faster or slower pace than is able to support the critical mass of the material object changes the materiality of that object and its' associated balance and harmony with its' specific environment. In other words it becomes in danger of ceasing to exist. Since the Human body is genetically programmed for cell replacement, material or temporal existence is programmed or modelled to exist then not exist. This means that we are programmed to live, we learn, and then we die. During life, we extend our chances if we *learn* to live in balance and in harmony, in the flow of universal energy.

Does this mean that your Being ceases to exist when you die?

This is possible, if you think that everything that *you are*, including your innate consciousness, is no more than a critical mass system called the Human body that is constructed of nothing more than continuously recycled energy and if you then live in that way, only for yourself, out of balance with other created things. In other words, the Human part of the Being ceases to exist as a living form, like all other physical living things within the temporal world. Even mountains eventually die.

Alternatively, if you choose to be *worthy* of creation, some of the energy that was a part of *your life* is preserved, to sleep and then to return. If you are to return to Source, or as some would say God or Heaven, you *must* take *responsibility* for the choices you make, both within your *thoughts* and for all the *actions* that *you* take within *your life*, choosing 'to be, or not to be'.

Quoting Shakespeare's opening of Hamlet:

> *'To be, or not to be: that is the question:*
> *Whether 'tis nobler in the mind to suffer*
> *The slings and arrows of outrageous fortune,*
> *Or to take arms against a sea of troubles,*
> *And by opposing end them? To die: to sleep;*
> *No more; and by a sleep to say we end*
> *The heart-ache and the thousand natural shocks*
> *That flesh is heir to, 'tis a consummation*
> *Devoutly to be wish'd. To die, to sleep;*
> *To sleep: perchance to dream: ay, there's the rub;*
> *For in that sleep of death what dreams may come'.*

Be careful what you may wish for. Wishes and dreams, wishful thinking, can be manifested in the ether. Shakespeare was also a messenger.

Only you and you alone are responsible for how you *choose* to live *your* life, regardless of the multitude of tests and challenges that we must each face in each and every life, or to put it another way: *'to suffer the slings and arrows of outrageous fortune'*.

You cannot blame others, nor can you impose your will on others and ultimately be *sustainable*, because control over another is an expressed and conscious form of separation from another form of creation. Any separation within the whole of creation is a contradiction. This means that, by denying the free will of another, you cannot ultimately be a part of the creation of the One, and therefore your wish not to continue as a connected Being, as a part of the One, *will be granted*.

Love is for giving, and must ultimately include the forgiveness for *anything* that has happened to you. Did not the Christ say 'love your enemies'? It is the ultimate in learning and giving. As I will explain later, the past does not exist, therefore the memory of past wounds is nothing more than that, a memory, one that you can choose to let go of while not forgetting the lesson that life was trying to teach you, both as an individual Being and, as previously intended, a *connected and holistic* Being, both within the temporal world *and* between the temporal and spiritual realms.

You can also choose not to surrender, not to learn and through that process to fight this inevitability: '*Or to take arms against a sea of troubles, And by opposing end them? To die: to sleep; No more; and by a sleep to say we end*'. The choice to learn or not to learn from troubles is the price of free will in order to become worthy of eternity, the *to be* or *not to be*, the message of potential eternal life, accessed by understanding the intended nature of each and every Being and the development of one-self. Each is a mirror for the other.

We sometimes call the essence of our true Being the *soul*, the seed system of true Being. Many thoughts and dreams can be contained and processed within a quantum of energy, carried forward into the lifetimes of '*the thousand natural shocks*' of possibility and learning. Sometimes we falsely look outside of ourselves to realize that possibility.

When we as conscious Beings look for God outside of the material objects that we can see, we are missing the point at every level, whether this is at the level of quantum energy, the Human body or the Universe. God exists at every level because God is One and *is* every level, including all the levels of energy and creation, and therefore *within you* as a soul Being. This is analogous to the learning of the Olympic Games symbol, and of Shakespeare's Hamlet.

We are not alone in this understanding, nor is this entirely new thinking. Many others have had the knowledge that God is, has been and will always be immanent, the divine manifested in the temporal world, including Albert Einstein, an eminent scientist and pantheist. That is where Einstein derived his genius as we call it, transcending the duality with extra-ordinary thinking. His original thinking came from within him, and yet at the same time he was connected to an understanding of the observable nature of the cosmos that he could not possibly experience by touch, sight, smell, taste or hearing.

Christ (the Being) tried to get this message across in his time as Jesus (the Human). This message is shown in the New Testament of the Bible, Book of John, Chapter 14, Verse 6: 'I am the way, the truth, and the life. No one comes to the Father except through Me'.

Many people interpret this as Christ *being* someone on the outside, to guide them to see this, without taking responsibility for oneself.

What the Christ was messaging is perhaps best understood by saying the words as though they apply to you: *I am the way, the truth, and the life; no one comes to the Father except through me.* He was essentially saying: *be like me* and *you* will help others to come back to the Creator, and as I lead by example, so must you too. He was and is a true leader and avatar that *serves* followers, always helping people through their understanding of the message and what that means in terms of choice.

The Christ reinforced this message within the Book of John, Chapter 14, Verse 7: 'If you had known Me, you would have known My Father also; and from now on you know Him and have seen Him'. In other words God is within you and you within

God, or if you do not believe in that, good or love is within you and you are within love and good, because creation is love *being* given and therefore *very good.*

God created Human Beings with free will as part of the whole. The best analogy I can give you regarding relationship to the common good, God or The One, is that we are each like cells in a body. We can choose to be benevolent or cancerous within the life that we each live and therefore every choice that each of us makes will either add to or subtract from the whole. This duality makes every Being a part of God, along with the tests of life to see if each of us are worthy of that creation and *service* to The One.

The next time you look at someone, try to think 'although *they* may appear different to *me*, be at a different stage of their journey to me or have a different perspective, they are essentially the same as me and we can therefore make life easier and happier by helping each other on our respective journeys that will eventually lead to the same destination'. That thought would also make God smile. If everyone is part of that whole, then we best serve The One by serving and helping each other and one-another.

The search for the Christ within each Being begins with learning that each and every life, and the unique challenges that are presented, will give each of our conscious free wills the opportunity to learn how to reconnect and pass through the *Gates of Light*, or 'steps' on the stairway to Heaven.

If and when you pass through all the Gates of Light, through the learning and sacrifice of the 'self' within 'one-self', you will come to know that Lao Tse, Siddhartha Gautama, Jesus, Mohammed and Nanak Dev are the same connected Being, with essentially the same message of *self-less love.* In spiritual circles he is known as *The Messenger*, because he carries the essence of the same message.

His *Being* will come again in the year 2,536 A.D. to help the learning and complete the experiment within the garden that we call Earth. This is the basis of the seven churches within the Bible's Book of Revelation. An eighth will follow.

*Learning teaches.*
*It is the perfect learning model.*


# 3. WHY ARE WE HERE?

'*WHY ARE WE HERE?*' is a question that Human Beings have been asking themselves since consciousness created awareness that they were and are part of a larger whole, The One, whether this is known as God, Nature or the Universe.

So is there a simple answer?

The simplest answer that I have is this: We are here to recognize the soul Being in others, which was *created for the same reason as our own.*

What makes this potentially more complicated is that we should also try through our thoughts and actions to help others on their journey, as though it has the same importance as our own journey, incorporating the importance of the messages that came before. *What is the point in reconnecting with God if not reconnected with one-another first?* The ultimate paradox is the con-artist ('con' ironically means 'with'). Deception serves no-one and consequently has no sustainable purpose. Therefore self-deception is ultimately meaningless. To quote Elizabeth I, "They are most deceived that trust most in themselves". The *unseparated* Divine connects all and everything.

Have you ever thought about the words 'Jesus died on the cross for our sins'? This could be interpreted as 'Jesus will save us'.

There is perhaps a more *poignant* message in this: 'Jesus, a Human who tried to help other people and undoubtedly did through the message and the Christ *Being*, was murdered by crucifixion because of the separation of others whom He called His children'.

The first interpretation can have the stain of abdication; the latter has a dye of responsibility. His death was not an isolated injustice; complete innocents have died and suffered since because of the separation of Human Beings, both directly and indirectly. Think of the young children at Auschwitz. His core message was to love one another. This has never changed, nor ever will. If Jesus the Christ, the will of God incarnate, was indeed murdered, then it was also by definition an attempt to kill God.

There have been many attempts to kill off God since, most commonly by 'scientific' writers. This I think God would object to. However, I do not think that God would think anything of experiencing temporal death as a loving Creator in order to protect the innocent, because the circle of life is eternal so ultimately it would make no difference. The first is the *last*, seeing the possibility of the outside from the inside; the alpha and the omega, seeing the possibility of Human Beings as His or Her creation.

Consequently, the latter interpretation of the message takes nothing away from Jesus' temporal death or the manner of death. The point is this: 'Jesus will save you' suggests that we can each find a saviour outside of ourselves. The way of life that the Christ and the other avatars *taught* is one of finding our true selves and taking responsibility for our lives, thoughts and actions. He taught *be like me*, and *follow by my example* in *helping others*.

That is our choice, for each and every one of 'us'.

The question might then be this: If that is the case, why do I sometimes suffer if I try to help others?

At a personal level, my journey was painful and has always been very uncomfortable, but I have always found the strength one way or another to never give up and to overcome my potential fears. What I have learned I share freely, both professionally and personally. I enjoy nothing more than helping and encouraging others to learn and grow. My advice is never to stop *helping*. Eventually both the truth and the learning from sharing and helping others will reveal itself. Fear will always be overcome.

Compare any fear or discomfort to learning to ride a horse. You might need some initial instruction, some help, or you could try to work it all out yourself. You might also need some encouragement. Courage is doing something despite your potential fears; encouragement is helping others overcome theirs. It is easier if you have something previous to go on, someone to lead, something to follow. To learn to ride you also have to risk falling off. Supposing that you do fall off, it might actually hurt. What do you do then: Give up, or get back on and try again? The cause of the pain is the process of learning, because your journey of learning is incomplete. Maybe you are the one helping another to ride that horse.

You might consider that the initial pain is not caused as a result of something that you have done, but by the actions of others. Firstly, if that is the case, then it proves the point about separation from others. How can we expect others to be different if we are not prepared to accept changes to and within ourselves *for others*? Secondly, how can they start to learn if not starting with the experience of you and your way of Being, the choices that you make that inspire others. Maybe you are here as the one to start helping them. Maybe you *are* that *mirror*, the one who helps to lead others by example.

Sometimes you will see others prosper at your expense, but this is always transient. To quote the words of Mahatma Gandhi, '*When I despair, I remember that all through history the way of truth and love has always won. There have been tyrants and murderers and for a time they seem invincible, but in the end, they always fall - think of it, always.*' Sometimes I prefer Groucho Marx's amusing quote: 'Time wounds all heels'. This can sound a little harsh, however it is essentially the same as *karma*. This also works the other way round, when you help others the favour is ultimately returned - just don't expect instant results! It might take some time, but what goes round really does come round. The circle is eternal.

The point is this: *All life is a test*. The test is for the long run. For each test we must prepare, much like we have to prepare for professional, vocational and academic examinations, and to do that we must all *learn*.

Some believe that we learn through successive lives. Is this true? I have spoken to people who have had hypnotherapy regression. During this experience they became aware of the existence of another life. When they researched this life they found an accurate correlation with what had been revealed to them. I too am aware of such lives. I think it is better that you pray that this is true, since to learn everything you need to know within a single lifetime might be too much for even the strongest and most resilient Human Being!

If you are content with the thought that this life is your one and only time, then that is your response and your choice alone. If you are incorrect then that is your responsibility also. Everyone that has become conscious of that choice has the opportunity to choose, possibly more than once in each lifetime. The reason this choice is so important now is that we are fast approaching the end-game and going into a new world. Regardless of the choice that you and only you can make, the primary lesson we must all ultimately learn is that we are each soul Beings, a part of a whole, or The One. At the very least, that must ultimately include a *common good* and a *respect* for all Beings in order to make the existence of *Human Beings* sustainable. We are conscious of sustainability, a thoughtful way of Human *Being*. We are not just a Human *Doing*.

In addition, there are many other thoughtful lessons that can be and *need* be learnt during life to help us *grow* as Human Beings. These can be learnt through new experience, by applying innate knowledge (using feelings or instincts), by asking questions and observing what is sustainable, by reflecting on our own behaviours using the mirror of others, through conscious thought or reason, and by sharing knowledge and the experience of others. In my experience, the best learning is gained through the deeply shared experiences of collaborating, creating and giving, because we then also have the benefit of the lessons, experience and knowledge of others, including their uncomfortable learnings, breakthroughs and accomplishments.

Pain involves pushing the boundaries, realizing that none really exist until you break through them. Essentially this is within the mind, enabling both the mind and body to grow, within the virtue of excellence.

One of the main lessons to learn from pain is healing. The word *disease* both literally and essentially means *dis-ease*, that something is not correct, whole or complete within either the physical / temporal, spiritual or psychological body. Modern medicine has an important part to play in the well-Being of every Human, and all other living creatures. It is part of Human technology and learning. However, medical research will one day identify and acknowledge that all healing is a change in energy, which creates and flows through the form of the Human body.

Let me give you a specific example to help explain. I was diagnosed many years ago with hypertension, or high blood pressure. This basically means a constriction of the arteries that increases the pressure on the heart to pump blood around the body. Some of this can be caused by stress, but often it is triggered by hereditary factors in one's genetics. Certain drugs can help relieve this pressure. How they work is by re*forming* the internal shape or flexibility of the arteries. Since all form is the shape of energy, it must be creating a change in energy within the body.

The ancient Egyptians understood this technology and practiced both holistic medicine and physical brain surgery. Hieroglyphs at the temple of Kom Ombo on the River Nile showed the surgical instruments the ancient Egyptians used, which were very similar to those used in modern times. Very few things are new. I remember something my father-in-law said to me. He said, 'Steve, there is nothing that you and I have thought of that is new, it is just that we have better technology now to make it happen'. In this, we can include the technology of language; same message, different language.

Traditional Chinese medicine, in development for over 4,000 years, uses this same understanding of the nature of energy. For example, acupuncture, chiropractic and reflexology and are simply different techniques to exploit the same technology (or know-how) of energy manipulation and redirection. Reflexology itself was invented and practiced over 5,000 years ago in ancient Egypt. It was only resurrected in the western world by William Fitzgerald in the 20th Century - again the process of *sharing* knowledge, things that are already *known* by someone, whether past or present.

Can anyone be a healer? The answer depends on at which level.

Just by active listening to someone and helping another through difficult times, you are being a healer. You could take this to a different level and perhaps be a doctor, nurse, counsellor or psychotherapist. However, the easiest way to being a healer is to be there for others in time of trouble. We can all learn to do this.

We must also learn to heal past wounds between two souls, to be at peace with one another. Soul healing can be from past lives, karma that is brought forward. During recent years I have reconnected with everyone that I needed to. There is peace between us, and nothing more to apologize for. Some of these people I recognize that I had known over many lifetimes. Some of these reciprocated the recognition. When you develop the gift, you will recognize these people, maybe including who you both were during that life and how you were related to each other. At one time or another, we all loved each other.

This may be difficult to accept, but when someone who does not deliberately bear you ill will does something to you that you would rather they did not, that is a lesson you must learn by reflection because you have not fully learnt from a similar experience it in the past. This might even be the same soul Being from the past upon whom you have inflicted a similar pain. This will also work in reverse for any positive experience or karma, when favour is ultimately returned and comes back to you.

If you doubt this, try apologizing to someone who you think has done harm to you, that you want this act to be in the past where it belongs. The apology is because you have made a judgement upon them, without really knowing them and what may have driven them to it. The reaction is usually unexpected. Even if you cannot forget, or are not supposed to as an important lesson, you can always forgive. Love is *for giving*; forgiveness is the ultimate healing for everyone, the message and promise of the Christ.

The lesson of healing is one of giving comfort and support during life. It can be applied to those who are experiencing pain or trying to find their way in life, the afflicted or disabled, the ill or dying, the homeless, the destitute or the starving, or even more simply the hungry, either physically or just in respect of the love that they need.

All Human Beings that have passed the second Gate of Light also become spiritual healers, working at a higher level of energy. This is fully manifested at the fifth Gate of Light (see Chapter 8).

The other lesson is to learn how to teach what we know. There is not much to say, except to share what you know for others' benefit. Do not force this upon them, rather let them choose to understand and challenge. The aim is not to win; there can be no losers in sharing. If you are correct, the challenge will reinforce the understanding or knowledge. If not, then it can be refined. However, walk away from someone who is vexatious or antagonistic until they acknowledge that you are doing this to try to help them. It is impossible to help someone unless they choose that want to be helped. By far the best form of teaching is leading by example.

I have often been asked by different people if the dynamics of life are driven by free will or fate (destiny). The best answer I can give is through an analogy.

Imagine, if you will, a ship sailing from England to the Americas. The ship is sailing from A to B whether the passengers like it or not. This is fate. Conversely, we are like the passengers on the ship. Our safety relies upon the ship. We can choose to do what we want while the ship is sailing, but the ship is still sailing from A to B. This is free will. We can choose to help keep the ship afloat or sink it. If the ship is in trouble, we can then choose to help others through it.

You might say that you do not find that ships are that safe, therefore let's use another example.

Imagine a blue and green planet. It will continue to revolve and move in an orbit around its' sun, as long as its' sun, moon and other orbiting planets continue supporting it. That is fate. We are free to do what we want on that planet, the *ship* that we rely upon to survive. That is free will. If we choose to sink that ship, how it keeps us alive, we will also perish. The gift of life will be taken away.

The same thoughts can apply to communities, those environments that are larger than us and commonly or *communally* good. Inclusive communities fall into the same purpose, as do organizations that are *benevolent* and inclusive, including consideration of their environments that make them *sustainable*. Our sustainability is therefore also part of our free will choice of *respect for something that is larger than us as individuals.*

There is a greater journey taking place, and we can only be a part of it, including our free will choices during each and every journey of life.

The final lesson to learn therefore is *service*; how to serve and be of service to others. It is the same as the service to The One. That is not the same as being subservient, especially to those who would wish to take away empowerment or have control over others. The love of One will never be like this, never taking away our choice. That is how you will recognize conscious separation in others.

Paradoxically, the more control you give up to the Universe (the ship or God) the more control you ultimately have over your own safe outcome. In Islam this means *surrender*. Understand this apparent puzzle and you will solve the puzzle of life itself.

Our thoughts and actions support the outcome, whether this is to make existence sustainable or transient. Our transience as *Human* Beings is illustrated by this. If the history of the Earth is concentrated into a twenty-four hour period, Human Beings have only been here for the equivalent of a few seconds. The test of the Universe, or creation, is therefore about choosing *good intentions* in the here and now to create *sustainable* outcomes for all life of Earth, and other sentient Beings in particular.

All other life creates harmony and balance within the whole, a symbiosis that sustains life itself. Without equilibrium there is no sustainability, yet according to Heraclitus, there is nothing permanent except change. The whole of creation is therefore a balancing act; the Buddha's *Middle Way* can be applied to so many things. For example, have we inherited the Earth from our ancestors, or have we borrowed it from our children? Do we sustain and share that which has been given or try to control it for ourselves? That is the choice we must all make for Human Beings to *be* and sustain.

The Universe is full of irony in this respect. A world built on barter tokens (money) can *never* be sustainable. How can a barter token be more important than that which it represents, the value of the object being shared? How can a system that is based on competition for money possibly work? Do you trade or compete over the ability to trade?

Money is a technology that represents our collaborative bartering system. Therefore this system should be owned by all, never by a few, for the benefit of all, to enable trade and reinvestment in collaborative, constructive and benevolent projects, and nothing else. I probably understood this irony better than most, having qualified as an accountant and earning a Masters degree in business administration, majoring in finance and technology.

While putting the finishing touches to this book, I received a message. The message was this: all humanity's problems are based on *greed*. Personal greed (taking more than you need) then results in corruption and then a pursuit for power. Power is then executed using the technology of money (or its' barter token equivalent), which then promulgates greed, etc. This is a non-virtuous circle (and unsustainable, as people will discover). With modern communications technology, very few have the excuse not to be able to understand this.

You can see that the circle can be broken at any time, at any of the stages. Greed is a dark energy that can exist within any Human Being. It is part of the shadow, the test. The greed can be jealousy of what another has, control over others rather than accepting their free will, power rather than empowerment, or having the root of evil as your goal - money for money's own sake. Money is simply a man-made technology to facilitate trade without having to carry the goods around. Can it be stored? It depends on what you put your faith in.

You might ask, therefore, if it is acceptable to accumulate a barter token (money). The only answer I can give you is that it depends on how it is earned and accumulated, and then how it is used and shared. If the barter token is earned and accumulated collaboratively to create flexibility (and a buffer) for a community that includes all within the community, and is then deployed constructively and benevolently across communities, then the use of money is moral. This is not advocacy for any particular political system: communism failed humanity as much as capitalism, because both were ultimately based on the control of others and the self-serving power of the few, and yet, both ironically and idealistically, these political systems had the same moral aims of being collaborative, constructive and benevolent for the *common good*. Fairness and freedom can only be underpinned by a moral system and *shared global values* in order to remain *sustainable*, regardless of any advocated political, sociological or economic system that claims to benefit the *common* good.

Systems of trade are shared and intrinsically collaborative. Other than for greed, control and ultimately self-serving power, I think that normally caring Human Beings accumulated the barter token because they were uncertain about their own future. They were uncertain about that future because of previous separation, and the assumed unwillingness of others to look after and share with them in later life. This also applied to anyone without the full ability to survive and avoid hunger in a world based on the management of limited resources, or economics.

Economics means the management of scarce resources (from the Greek *oikonomia, or* household administration). Economic 'growth' is therefore an oxymoron, a contradiction. You cannot manage the 'growth' of something that is scarce or limited in supply. However, you can make something that is limited in supply better serve the needs of everyone through efficiency and effectiveness in the processes of production, trade and service.

Many years ago, to help understand and solve this apparent problem, I thought about the analogy of baking a cake. Suppose that the cake is fixed in size, and you take a larger and larger slice of the cake. The outcome is that others will end up with less. If they end up with less than they need, there will be conflict. There is more to trade than money. The natural and physical resources of the planet are finite. The thinking, conceptual and technological solutions of Human Beings are not.

So what is the solution? The answer is to bake a more nutritious cake, something with greater *value* to *everyone*, of lasting shared benefit that is sustainable, *by collaborative effort*. That does not entail baking a larger cake than is needed, because that will result in waste and impact the environment upon which all life depends, including the existence of Human Beings. Nor does it mean consuming more than you would need, because there is only so much you can eat without also wasting it. As Gandhi once put it, *there is enough for need but not for greed.*

Our technology, the science of know-how, can be shared to benefit all. This is what we were taught at the beginning of the Masters degree: decide how to use what is learnt, a decision on how to help avoid the 'haves' and 'have not's'. This polarization is *not inevitable* unless we accept that greed is good. However, who would honestly elect leaders who believe in such a thing unless they were greedy themselves? I for one do not want my children to grow up in such a world.

The intentions for *sustainable* growth are manifested through our *collaborative* thoughts and actions. One is pointless without the other. We need to act on what we think, or they remain just thoughts. *Constructive* and *benevolent* outcomes, including consideration of the interests of future generations (of which you are likely to be a part if you are worthy and incarnate again), give us the motivation to go through this learning process together by *sharing* our good thoughts and actions with the same intent, creating a *holistic* and *virtuous* circle of pragmatic and spiritual growth.

Learning is about growth and sharing. This can be applied to healing, teaching and serving others. Ultimately it is personal, enabling a return to Source and survivability.

Sharing gives all of us a common purpose and something of lasting shared value and joint benefit; it provides the basis of a perfect learning model. It also gives us hope for life, together, a life that is authentic and sustainable. Conversely, life will go on, whether Human Beings exist or not.

*Pain means that something is*
*not whole or complete.*

# 4. LIFE

AT THE AGE OF 15, my father died. He was 39 years old. I was the one who found him. He was hanging by the neck. His name was Alan.

When I touched his hand it was cold and felt like wax. You can imagine how I felt as a 15 year old. I was neither a man nor a child who had found his father dead in violent circumstances. You can imagine, but you cannot truly *know* until you have experienced it. This is true of any situation.

We, including my mother and younger sister, never spoke about my father again for thirty-five years. When I gave my sister away to be married twelve years after my father had died, my brother-in-law did not even know his name.

I finally talked to my mother about my father and what had happened when I was fifty years old. During that conversation it was clear that she still carried a lot of pain about what had happened, as we spent much of that hour talking about how she felt. In truth I had wanted to talk to her about how we had both felt for all those years. I just did not have the courage. It was just before the start of The One Project that I knew I had to deal with this, to clear this taboo subject and help the soul healing that was required.

Before I recovered from the experience of talking about it, I confess that I quickly descended into the depths of despair, the abyss, the darkest place you can ever experience, before starting to recover and learning from the experience. I now describe this as a transformational breakdown, followed by a *transformational breakthrough*, the self-imposed limits of my mind. In other words, I had to go through an enormous pain barrier in order to learn and grow, many years after his death, and it started with the courage to confront the darkness, both within and without. To quote Winston Churchill, 'If you are going through hell, just keep going'.

If you lose someone to what appears to be suicide you can blame yourself, thinking what would have happened *if* only I had done something different. My sister, then only thirteen years old, said one of the wisest things I have ever heard: 'If is such a big word, and yet so small'.

Incredibly, I found out not long after talking to my mother about it for the first time that one of my uncles, one of my father's brothers, had actually felt the same way, that he had also blamed himself for what had happened. Had he known the circumstances, he would have changed them. He revealed this sentiment for the very first time at his wife's funeral. He had carried a similar pain to mine for the same thirty-five years. Experience of another's death, especially those close to us, has a strange way of revealing how we feel about life and life's events, and what we feel we should and could have done during life.

Pain tells you that something is not correct, that something is incomplete, or that something needs changing. You cannot mask pain with something positive, like an air-freshener covering up a nasty smell, because the underlying cause of the pain remains. To avoid pain is unrealistic. To avoid dealing with it and learning from the experience you deceive no-one except yourself.

Each of us must first understand the cause of the pain, which is within us, because it is ours and ours alone. Then, through a deep understanding and acceptance of the change within you from what you have *learned*, the pain will disappear as though it no longer exists. As the Dalai Lama once put it, invite suffering to make it disappear.

If something no longer appears to exist, then it will not exist. There is a new perception, an additional learning, and a new reality. *No pain* from what you have learned becomes the new reality. I will share some of the things I learned later, mainly about pain and its' relationship to love. First, I will share a universal truth.

The circumstances of each life are *how* each soul learns, and will therefore grow. Each life is unique; therefore each and every *learning process* is unique, including understanding something positive from the death of my father, which impacted everyone who knew him in different ways. Each time the circumstances and the individual perception are different, in each and every life, until all the required learning of the nature of life, death and creation is manifested and understood within each and every soul.

When this happens, a return to Source, to God (or the common good), is possible. Except with this also comes the realization that service to Source is also a service to others, and that helping and supporting others is the ultimate honour and therefore *serves* the ultimate good. By this, the will of God is manifest and fulfilled. This is the basis of Universal intention, which I will cover in Chapter 9.

Therefore the enlightened always choose to come back until all worthy souls have learned to serve each other and help one another through each and every life. I have learnt many important lessons through the experience, words and wisdom of others, past and present, who were also prepared to share.

So what did I learn from the death of my father?

Apparent suicide or murder are two of the worst forms of death, mainly because they seem to defy explanation. I now know that taking one's own life relates to a lack of self-worth, connection with others and a love of one-self, and is not meant to be, even if the person is in deep pain. Taking the life of another, no matter how seemingly justified, is also an ultimate form of control that is not meant to be, and therefore cannot be justified. If life was given to Humanity, it is not Humanity's right, nor any individual's, to take it away. When someone wants revenge, even if driven by abject pain, the test is to resist becoming the same as the original perpetrator. These were key lessons in many.

However, I only learned the first lesson relating to suicide fully thirty-five years later when my eldest daughter and her fiancé lost a dear friend who had taken his own life in his early twenties. This means that the learning can take many years, and sometimes only with the benefit of reflecting on information shared and received through the related and connected experience of others.

When I spoke to my daughter about her experience, I asked her how she felt. She said that she regretted something: she had not told her friend that she loved him while he was still alive and that if all his friends had told him how special he was to them that he might not have done what he did. I asked her if she had learned anything from this. She replied by saying that from now on she would tell all those she loves how important they are to her.

It does not matter how someone died, or the circumstances of their death. We must learn to forgive each other and for what happened to them. I also learned to forgive myself, and from

40

that moment the pain of my father's death disappeared. The barrier had been broken through, because I had learnt what I truly needed to understand. To forgive someone else, we must first learn to forgive ourselves and how we feel. None of us are, or have been, without sin (or separation).

I am proud of my eldest daughter, Claire, to have had the courage to say that, and in doing so I think she may have taught many of us a valuable lesson. If what she said is true, and we can all learn from this experience, then neither her friend's nor my father's deaths were in vain. Their deaths were part of the circle of life which is here to teach us *how* to live, with others in mind, that their innate need for belonging and to be loved are no different to our own. Given the choice, we must never take another's life.

I also remember something my grandfather told me just a few weeks before he died of cancer.

We were in Spain on a family holiday and my father, sister, an uncle and I had been horse riding together for several hours in the hot sun on very hard leather saddles. When we arrived back at the hotel, my uncle, who had been wearing thin cotton shorts, was walking with his legs apart and couldn't sit down properly without wincing. At dinner that evening I asked my grandfather if he would go horse riding with us the next day. He made us laugh when he replied, "No, I have learnt Ross's lesson". Ross was my uncle's name.

Wouldn't it be great if we could actually learn from others' mistakes? Unfortunately we sometimes have to learn the lesson ourselves, from our own experiences. My grandfather was a very wise man. He was a professional soldier in the Second World War, and risked his life many times. I never understood then why he was so wise. I do now.

That was the last family holiday all of us had together, as within just over two years my family lost my grandfather, grandmother and my father, my father exactly two years after my grandfather's death. When my grandfather died, I cried for week. When my grandmother died, I had trouble crying, even though we were so close. When my father died, I could not cry for six months. That is the nature of pain that is individual and cannot be shared, our own life's journey from which we must learn.

*So why does God allow pain?* - So that we can learn about love.

*Why does God want us to learn about love?* - So that we can become like Him or Her, forgiving of all.

*Why does God want us to become like Him or Her?* - So that God can be fulfilled, manifest within us, as a part of us, as One.

We separate to learn how to unify, keeping that which is sustainable as individuals. Love is the super-glue. This little poem might help an understanding of how we can all learn about life and each other:

> *I think what this is all about,*
> *The way it's meant to be:*
> *At one with all upon this Earth,*
> *Enough of 'you' and 'me'.*

Learn to do what you can for others, when you can, while they are still alive. Then you will be able to understand the purpose of life, and in the process to find your higher self.

Through this, you will also find your own reconnection with Source, which is the same thing for all of us and within all of us. After all, pure love is when someone or something is more important than one-self, by seeing one-self, and others, without the 'self'.

*There is nothing wrong with two sides to everything. Perception sees both.*

# 5. DUALITY

MANY PEOPLE HAVE SAID TO me that they do not believe in anything outside of the world that they cannot access and understand beyond the five senses of touch, smell, taste, sight and hearing. Yet, if you were for example a shark, you would be able to sense other living creatures and shapes through electro-magnetic energy. What if Human Beings could also similarly sense *unseen* energy?

The truth is we can, for example, when we feel the difference between hot and cold objects, get sun-burned after spending too much time in the sun, or receive an electric shock from static electricity!

We also have electro-magnetic activity within our brains that can be monitored using specialized technology, for example Electroencephalography, or EEG, which measures the ionic currents within the neurons of the brain. This type of energy that we call electro-magnetic activity is partially how thoughts are manifested and created, and is the first sign of the apparent duality of the brain and the mind. However, everything in the Universe is formed from energy, including our bodies, our brains and what we can then create with them.

Since thoughts and the brain are made from the same stuff that we call energy, this duality is merely a distinction so that we can identify different components or effects within the same system. We sometimes call this system the *mind*.

What is duality?

Duality is when something exists at the same moment with the same essence as something else. Energy can manifest in many forms and at different levels at the same time. The material brain (or the Human body) and the thoughts of the mind (or feelings) are a good example of this duality.

The connection with the higher self is another form of the duality of existence itself. The genius of Rene Descartes was shown in his famous quote 'Cogito ergo sum', 'I think therefore I am'. He did not merely understand this, he divined and then *knew* by the purity of its' revelation. *Thinking* cannot be analysed because it is a way of *Being*. Conversely, *Being* cannot be analysed because it is a way of *thinking*. The quote defies analysis because it is *pure* and *holistic* thinking from a conscious Being, *aware of its' own consciousness and existence*. That which is pure needs no distinction.

The forms of duality are not only discrete through the understanding given by semantic language, but they are also continuous from the infinitesimal to the infinite, and vice versa. The distinction within duality is merely a tool of language to compare systems or concepts, to give them each a name that is easier to communicate to one another by making them *artificially* and *temporarily* discrete within the Human mind.

A system is simply something of interest to the mind that is made up of its' essential parts or components. Each system is part of a larger environment. If you add or remove any component within any particular system, the behaviour of the system will change. The system both consumes inputs and excretes outputs, interacting with its' environment.

To help understand this, I will give three illustrative examples of systems that are at the same time discrete in language terms *and* continuous in terms of the same energy being constructed at different levels or in different forms.

The first is how structure is created through essential components, for example quantum mechanics (physics), molecules (chemistry), DNA (biology), the Human body, organizations, cultures and ultimately civilizations, beliefs and value systems. Each builds upon another to a level of critical mass system; either that or each is a component of a larger environment, depending on your perspective.

The second example is a rainbow. Rainbows are created when light waves are diffracted by water vapour, creating a discretely observable spectrum of colours from white light which consists of all colours (the whole). Each 'colour' has a wave frequency, including those we cannot see directly with the Human eye.

Human Beings can usually see red, orange, yellow, green, blue, indigo and violet, but not all the 'colours' that are created can be seen by Human Beings with the naked eye, for example infra-red (below the wave frequency of red) and ultra-violet (beyond the wave frequency of violet). However, some Beings can see and respond to these other 'colours', for example honey bees that can 'see' ultra-violet light. Human Beings can also 'see' this energy frequency by observational thinking, for example when ultra-violet light is reflected back from a white material object. These 'colours' can also be dually described as being both waves (frequencies) and particles (binary digits), indicated by the digitization of colours using computing technology. Yet all manifestations of 'colour' are also part of white light which contains all colours.

The third example is more holistic: space (*no thing*), energy, form, solar systems, galaxies and the Universe (everything).

You can see how within each of these examples that the components are both interdependent and connected in terms of the form and their environment, or levels of critical mass. The thing that all three examples have in common is that the systems and components are all made from the same or similar energy, but that each system *also* exists in its' own right, in its' own space. Each is also part of a larger whole (except the Universe, which is *everything*, or all words). Everything is connected at all levels and within all dimensions.

Each system builds upon another or, looked at the other way round, can be deconstructed into its' core and essential components. Everything consists of an organized, organic and interdependent system, each part observed and created or defined within the *mind*. However, these boundaries are also temporary and therefore transient semantics within the mind, another duality.

It is possible that something can exist as a fact for a moment in time, but only that which is true can be sustainable. The truth is a succession of these facts that are of temporary form that can be re-organized to create any possibility, the organized mind of God. The artificially discrete (or temporary form) and the seamless continuity of re-usable energy are therefore observations of the same thing or phenomena within the mind. Looked at from one perspective, it is Human language and imagination. Looked at from another, it is the mind of God. The duality of the perfect model for experiment and learning is the same no matter which way round you look at it.

The duality of God is immanent in everything. Consciousness is *both* the mind of God *and* energy observing its' own form. We are a part of God, the whole or the One, and part of the One is within us; as above, so below.

Yes, this is circular thinking, otherwise how could we have the concept of eternity, the symbol ∞ for infinity, the symbol 8, or two *no things*, the 0 and 0 duality, conjoined or manifested? The only thing you can say about a circular argument is that it is not linear. What you can say though is that it is continuous and sustainable, able to grow through a virtuous circle, an expanding Universe, at least until *this* experiment is complete. Then it improves or starts again, learning from the outcomes of each model. Created Beings are part of this experiment, to see what works, what is sustainable, including free will consciousness and choice.

The interesting thing about love is that it requires no *initial* thought. It can be manifested through pure *Being*. This shows that love is *pure*, that it does not have to be thought into existence. It already existed at the very beginning of creation, because creation *is* love *and* a way of *Being*. If love existed from the beginning and can be felt in any situation, then love must be within everything. Whether or not we are conscious of this does not change this sustainable truth. We become aware of these sustainable truths through consciousness and experience.

Is the mind the same as consciousness?

I thought about this long and hard after reading a well-researched book on medical science into the nature of consciousness. I only made the connection when I realized the self-evident truth: consciousness is energy observing its' own form. This eureka moment was a real awakening of my own consciousness. I will try to explain this in a different way to help understand the timely transformation of Human consciousness that is taking place.

Please try to imagine a goldfish bowl. Now imagine a single goldfish swimming around inside the bowl. Is the goldfish conscious of its' own existence? I cannot answer that question because I am not a goldfish!

However, *imagine* that you are that goldfish. You would probably sense and be conscious of the environment that you live in and perhaps not much else, except perhaps for the edge of the goldfish bowl and the hand that comes down to feed you. This is the *first level of consciousness* and the first *connection* that you make with the whole.

Now imagine another goldfish within the same bowl with the same level of consciousness. Not only might you be able to sense that it was the same species, but with your thoughts in the form of *empathy*, you might be able to imagine how that goldfish has similar thoughts and feelings to you. This is the *second level of consciousness* and the second *connection* with the whole. At this point you might also acknowledge that the other goldfish is similar to you, but you do not yet *know* that it is the same as you (currently a very strange thought!).

The world outside of the goldfish bowl that you inhabit is a world of possibility, except that you cannot access this directly *except by thought*. If you were conscious of your environment, and your environment's environment, you might then be able to imagine a world outside of that goldfish bowl. This is the *third level of consciousness*, when you become aware that there is an overall environment that *sustains* you and is the third *connection* that you make with the whole, the whole environment of The One. Early types of worship took this form, even if this awareness only stretched as far as a Sun or Moon which could be seen with the naked eye.

Now imagine that there is another Being outside of the goldfish bowl looking at *you* (and incidentally the other fish in the same bowl with you). This perspective is important because it is how we are seen by other Beings that are not in the same environment, including Human Beings from other faith systems or communities. If you could see the perspective of all the Beings at the same time and treat them as you would wish to be treated, the *main* message of the Christ, you will have made the *fourth* connection. This is sometimes also called the *fourth dimension*.

Dimensionality is how space is created so that 'discrete' forms of energy can be described within it. When energy collaborates at different levels it creates form or material objects, but as we know, energy also travels between them. There are many examples of this and I am sure that you could think of a few more. The examples I will give are: Light from stars in the Universe to the Human eye, micro-waving food and radio broadcasting.

If the Human mind recognizes this and the Being receiving the gift is worthy of the gift, then Human minds can collaborate not just by sharing thoughts through words, but also through the mind directly, a connected Universal mind. Some people already have a gift such as this which some might call psychic ability, clairvoyance, remote viewing or telepathy. Many other Human Beings may suspect that it exists, including possibly through having a Tarot reading, which is based on the Jewish Kabbalah, literally meaning 'receiving'. Even playing cards are based on this system, often used by Romany Gypsies as a means of divination. Both groups were targeted by the Nazis, partially because of this spirituality and knowledge and the perceived threat that it presented.

Do you suspect that such 'receiving' is possible? For example, have you ever intended connecting with a person when that person was about to do the same thing? Have you ever been somewhere that looks familiar to you but you have not been there before? Alternatively, have you ever had a déjà vu about a particular situation? Perhaps the most common is when you meet someone and quickly or immediately feel an inexplicably strong bond or *connection* with the other person, to the extent that feel that you *know* that person better, certainly within a much shorter space of time, than others with whom you have been acquainted with for much longer. However, do not get too hooked up on these thoughts at the moment as this is not a good place for a fish to be!

This gift also manifests through energy healing, to which those who have experienced *Reiki* will testify. The Christ was a known healer, with gaps in history when it is not fully known what it was that Jesus was learning. His ministry only lasted a couple of years. There is evidence that there was a connection with the same region as the Buddha. As a member of the Jewish faith and as an adept healer, there would also have been knowledge of the Kabbalah, if mot mastery of it. Through parable, Jesus had said to Simon and the others, *"Fear not; but follow me, and I will make you from this time fishers of men."*

At times we can be nothing more than fish in our own little world, not caring about others and our connection and interdependency with 'them'. That is a thought worth correcting, one that only each of 'us' can choose.

I need to introduce the Human *concept* of 'time'. Each time has its' moment. I will state this as clearly as I possibly can: *time does not exist*. 'Of course it does!', you might exclaim. However, I will qualify this by saying that *time does not exist except as a concept*

50

*within the Human mind.* When Albert Einstein was asked what 'time' was he told them that it was what a clock said.

'Time' is a measure of change between point particles (or matter of fact). Materially observable energy waves are simply the rhythmic symmetry of movement of point particles as they are subject to the *Law of Attraction* in all directions. If they appear symmetrical in a linear fashion, this is because the observer is a line of sight between the push and pull impact of two or more point particles without significant lateral interference. In other words it only appears to be linear, as is evidenced by the fact that light can be 'bent' by the gravitational pull of a denser mass of point particles (for example a planetary body) or $E=MC^2$.

Genius has a more lucid perception of relationship with new ideals and possibilities (including the concept of God) because it is less clouded by bounded rational thought and more by clarity of view (the meaning of the word 'clairvoyance') or, put another way, by *insight* or the *sight within*. Einstein's mind never extended to explaining the concept of time, because he *knew* that it had no intrinsic meaning. You could argue whether or not insight is created by design or merely an accident, a coincidence. However, it is also true that insight has been both nurtured by society as a sustainable benefit, and sometimes condemned as heretical if it challenges the status quo, perhaps for the same reason. Coincidence is a duality.

*Insight* would also explain the genetic distribution of schizophrenia if the perceived boundaries between genius and madness were not readily differentiated by surviving groups who must have benefited, or perceived that they benefited, from the presence of such a member within their societal group. Those with *insight* helped save lives and therefore manifested a benefit to society.

So how can we explain the *concept* of 'time'?

Time is a measure of the change in form of objects, including the position of the hands on the clock.

We approximate the measurement of 'time' by commonly referring to a year (approximately one revolution of the Earth around the Sun), a month (approximately one revolution of the Moon around the Earth), and a day (one revolution of the Earth on its' axis in relation to the Sun). Yet these are not constant according to our calendars and so we have to adjust the calendar every few years. For example, extra days were added to create the both the Julian and Gregorian calendars. We also need to add an extra day to create a leap year every four years. The clock is merely a subdivision of these very approximate *measurements*. Even the atomic clock would need to be adjusted every few million years.

If you could ask animals that do not use calendars or clocks what the time was, the bemused answer would probably be *'now'*. Of course, some animals migrate with the seasons, but they migrate because they know things around them are *changing*. When we talk of time, we mean from *this time*, from *now* on. There is no time like the present can be restated as 'there is no time except the present'. People who have presence, those who fully engage with others, are always *present* in the here and *now*.

So why did Human Beings create the concept of time?

The answer is relatively simple: it was to help manage the available energy more efficiently and effectively. One of the original uses was to help anticipate the floods of the Nile in order to manage the production of food. We still have much to learn from (or remember the learning of) the technology of the ancient Egyptians.

So how would I describe the concept of time in relation to my own journey of learning, especially in relation to what we might call eternity?

Firstly, *the past does not exist* except as a memory stored in the memory of the Being, either currently within the mind as it is, or within what we might call the *soul* stored as *innate* knowledge.

You might question how the latter can be. I can tell you quickly now that I glimpsed *eternity and infinity* during this journey, this lifetime, at the age of 6, a long time before I started writing this down. Sometime in the future people will also come to know that they have been created on Earth to help other Human Beings, much as the Christ Being and the other avatars were.

Secondly, the future does not exist except as a *possibility* that is created within *intention* in the *here* and *now*.

Therefore, the best description I can give of the connection between the concept of time, eternity and infinity is through another analogy. Imagine a large, flat, circular disk with a small hole in the centre. Now imagine time as representing the changing form of objects travelling along the surface of the disk, recycling the energy from which the objects have been made, but at the moment travelling from the centre of the disc outwards.

What happens when 'time' reaches the 'edge' of the disc?

Imagine now that the recycled energy travels underneath the disc from the 'edge' of the disc back to the centre of the disc, and so on. Now you have a concept of eternity.

Now imagine expanding the surface of the disc 'up' and 'down' so that the midpoint of the radius of the disc is elevated and circular from the centre to the 'edge' (like a doughnut ring). The changing form of energy still moves from the centre to the 'edge' and back again. Only this time try to imagine that the energy moves progressively along the ring in both directions, covering all parts of the ring. It keeps on doing this, forever. Now you have a concept of infinity.

The disc itself can also represent space, energy and form, the whole of creation, with the creative Source, God, Jehovah, Allah or The One, at its' centre of creation. The *possibilities* of ultimate creation from the here and now are infinite.

Because of this *learning model*, eternity and infinity can be 'viewed' from any point on the disc in any direction of space or 'time'. The point from which it is viewed is exclusively at the *here* and *now*. Some Beings are connected at higher levels through the gift of 'receiving', of being able to see parts of the disc, in order to *help others*. That is why some Human Beings are psychic or clairvoyant, whether they are angelic or have been fallen angels. The fallen that have chosen not to return and *serve* other Beings lose the gift.

Human Beings have the gift to be conscious of their own existence, so the *basis* of the transformation of all Human consciousness has already been created.

We are all part of this creation, including our consciousness, which is why Human Beings are now ready for the *fifth connection* or *dimension*, the transformation of Human consciousness. This is where God fully manifests the will, the transformation of Human consciousness, access to the Christ Being within all, a time when there will be no more sorrow, no more pain. The awareness of this choice comes first; then all will be required to choose a path. You might need some more information before you can consider what this means. This is described in Chapter 8. More people will then earn the gift of 'receiving' through their service to others, with the choice to continue.

Remembering that all conscious Beings have free will, one of the main questions asked by conscious *Human* Beings, ever since becoming aware of the choices, pain and tests of life and how it affects them personally, can be summarized as follows:

*Is there a duality of good and bad, or could they be a part of the same thing?*

Put another way, *if God is love then why was bad created?*

The answer is that free will creates the bad, the choice between separation or connection. This is the price of free will.

Before *you* can resolve this in your mind, firstly ask yourself another question:

*Is it bad to have bad thoughts using your free will?*

Please ponder this question for a moment before reading on.

*What if I consciously then decide not to put such thoughts into action? Is that good or bad?*

All of us can have bad or negative thoughts at various moments. That is part of our free will. Anyone who says otherwise is either deceiving others or self-deceiving, ultimately the worst form of deception.

However, what we do with bad or negative thoughts is part of the test that enables spiritual and material progression. It is how we can learn from the perception of distinction towards the right way of living.

*If we have bad thoughts, or have had bad things done to us, should we pass that badness onto another?* Alternatively, *if we have had bad things happen to us, could we end that cycle by manifesting good for another, because we know better?*

While writing this book I met with a friend for a coffee in London. During the conversation she asked me if I thought I was a good person. I answered that it is not for me to judge, but for others to have an opinion on that based on what I do, based on my actions. She then asked me what I thought made someone a good person. I immediately answered that they would be collaborative, constructive and benevolent.

What I learnt from this is that a subjective opinion might be acceptable, but only sustainable values can be true and objective. We cannot claim to be good, because that is a subjective perspective that can have an alternative viewpoint. What we can do is aim for the ideal and try to be the best we can be in each and every moment, aiming to live within the values of morality. Conversely, if we have had bad things happen to us, we could end that negative cycle by manifesting good for another, because we *know* better, because we are aiming to be moral and objective.

The point is that we can acquire *knowledge* through learning, experience and shared values that create a *sustainable* outcome. An eye for an eye and a tooth for a tooth would only help opticians and dentists.

The Light casts a *shadow* that can create what we feel as *pain* so that we can 'see' where the Source of Light came from, enabling each of us, through our own free will, to choose to leave the shadow. The shadows appear time and time again, until we learn, or are individually decided unworthy because the learning has been resisted. In this process of direction, we each have to learn the purpose of moral value. We might turn the other cheek, but remember that we only have two. The time to choose has come.

Please ask yourself two more questions:

*Is it benevolent to have good thoughts with my free will?*

*What if I then consciously decide not to put such thoughts into action?*

Thinking good thoughts and then not consciously acting on them is 'waste' of energy. It is also immoral because it is not constructive and benevolent. This indicates that there is nothing intrinsically right or wrong with good or bad thoughts, it is our free will choice; it is what we do with them that matters, either through our actions or intentions for others, because that is how they manifest a sustainable and material outcome.

However, good and bad are *not* subjective, since morality is now understood in *The Book of Life*: destructiveness and selfish taking are not good actions; constructiveness and benevolence in both thoughts and actions are *intrinsically* good. However, our thoughts, decisions and actions cannot be completely objective without firstly considering these temporary distinctions. Unless we can rely upon innate knowledge of what we know is correct from our guiding conscience, which at the moment is not universally shared, global or Universal values are the only objective solution that free will Human Beings *can* share.

Therefore it is not only what you think that is essential, it is also what others think and value for the common good. Human Beings are in this together. Pious thoughts manifest little; creating positive intention and then putting them into action is an *essential* part of growth. How else can Human Beings become sustainable as distinct from extinct, and worthy of our lives on Earth for a return to Heaven, even if the Heaven is only created on Earth?

This should be within our thoughts as much as we each are capable within our individual shades of gray, but in any case morality must be within our *actions*, what we manifest in temporal reality, both constructively and benevolently. These are the ultimate choices we have: consciously do bad things, consciously do neither bad nor good things, or consciously be of service. These are our choice of Being.

These form the dualities within us. This is what creates the choice.

*Service is its' own reward:*
*Deception masks itself with deception;*
*love or contradiction removes the mask.*

# 6. SERVICE

SERVING BASED ON GIVING IS love. Service based on an expected reward is not. Service to the common good or The One is therefore an act of love.

There are those who might think that they are in the service of The One or the common good. Here are some questions that can be asked as to how strongly supportable this is, whether or not this is potentially self-deceiving:

a) *Who am I learning for: myself or one-self, ultimately to teach truth and meaning to others?*

b) *Who am I praying for: myself, or one-self that focuses on others?*

c) *Who am I meditating for: myself, or for reconnection with others and The One?*

d) *Do I think that there is only one path back to Source, which is my chosen way, and that those who would have the same intention to reconnect are wrong?*

e) *Who am I thinking about: myself, or one-self that focuses on others in need?*

f) *For whom am I acting: myself, or one-self that focuses on others?*

g) *What is my readiness to help others, by going out into the world, sharing what I know, and being prepared to be challenged in order to continue the learning?*

*h)* *What are my views on conflict; is conflict acceptable?*
*i)* *Does the change start in others or within one-self?*
*j)* *Have I made my peace with everyone, even those who have wronged me, based on my incorrect or incomplete perception or judgement of 'them'?*

To come up with the perfect set of answers is never easy, but that is the *choice*. The focus of service does not need to be on everyone. You do not know everyone. However, those already in your life are a good starting point. Whether or not a person belongs to a particular faith or has a particular belief system, the self-questioning is the same.

To be a person of the common good or God must necessarily be based on a desire for both positive thoughts and actions for all, which gives life and creation its' meaning. These must by definition include others *and* for The One, without any separation or *thought* of separation, and certainly without any focus on self-promotion or self-benefit that could *exclude* others.

Consider the disconnected examples of so-called philosophers and scientists who try to disprove the existence of The One, which serves no purpose which can be ultimately called common good, other than by falsely arguing that religious beliefs cause conflict, which I will address separately.

Firstly philosophers: philosophy literally means a love of wisdom. Since wisdom includes all things that can be known, it cannot exclude anything. The One represents the whole, including both reality and the process of creation; therefore it cannot exclude knowledge of the whole, which would deny the concept and therefore the existence of The One. That is illogical, since The One is everything.

The concept exists, so it must be true in reality. To say that the Human mind can create this without reference to creative energy does not make any sense. It is *nonsense*; it is *a posteriori* knowledge. The concept is also sensible with or without reference to prime movement in the act of creation, *which is pure energy to create form*. The concept is therefore also *a priori*. To look at this *either* as *a priori* or a *posteriori* in isolation is reducing the whole to something less than the whole, which makes no sense.

Relating this to Human Beings, which are certainly less than the whole, a computer can learn from itself and add to its' own development, but it also needs to be created and programmed to be able to do so in order to achieve this. I certainly do not think that Human consciousness was created from the mind of dinosaurs or early mammals! Since all evolutionary process must fulfil the purpose of filling available niches in nature, consciousness of one's own energy form serves no purpose for survivability, unless that survivability also relates to something of a higher order relating to that energy.

Secondly scientists: philosophy created a branch of philosophy that we now call science. The philosopher Pythagoras is sometimes known as the father of mathematics, an important branch of science based on numerology. All mathematicians owe much of what they understand and know to the life and work of Pythagoras.

Scientific method is based on a systematic observation of anything that happens, and then providing empirical and measurable evidence of the stated hypothesis relating to the verifiable truth of that observation. Since a system is a bounded set of components, it must by definition exclude anything that sits outside of the system, in other words its' environment or the whole. Analysing a system cannot presume to be able to synthesize or represent the whole, because the analysis is by definition a reduction of a defined system that can only be a sub-set of the whole, and that cannot possibly include the whole!

Each system has a critical mass that can be approximated by observing, identifying and describing its' critical components, or by measuring the content of its' component energy and dimensions by one scientific method or another. The critical mass defines the extent of the form of the object or the observed phenomenon in existence, which can be described at many different levels and in many different ways, even through the use analogies. In any case, these forms are connected to one another within broader connected systems or by energy connecting across different systems or dimensions from one form to another (transformation).

This energy connection is best described as the attractive energy between material objects. For example, through the important work of Isaac Newton, an eminent physicist and Professor of Mathematics (who was also a Pantheist), Human Beings can understand the concept and observable phenomenon of 'gravity'. Only disconnection can deny this. The fall of the apple was more than just apples.

According to Erwin Schrödinger, another eminent physicist and pioneer of quantum mechanics, the atomic weight of the Human body is the same as air, so if gravity was not true Human Beings would be floating in mid-air! Gravity as we sense it is simply the attractive energy between the critical mass of a Human body and the critical mass of the Earth. If the critical mass of neither existed, neither would be objects in their current form, and the energy would be used elsewhere.

If the Human body did not exist, the Earth could *continue* to exist, indicating that Human Beings are critically dependent upon the Earth and not the other way round. The Earth *is* our environment, and also a part of the whole. If Human Beings self-servingly abuse the Earth to the point of ecological and environmental imbalance, the existence of Human Beings is not sustainable. If Human Beings ever self-servingly decided to abuse the Earth and then used science technology to try to escape to another world, the Universe would also ensure that this is not possible. Morality is essential to create consensus and sustainability. Moral consensus would play its' part.

Scientists have much to add to the sum of Human knowledge, which is by definition incomplete otherwise there would be no more need for science! However, the only reason we listen to famous scientists is because they are famous *scientists*. To say that The One or God does not exist cannot be empirically evidenced, let alone proved or disproved by scientific method. Therefore the *opinion* of a scientist is of no more consequence than that of any other Human Being.

Some works and teachings are self-serving, and others are not. What distinguishes them is whether or not they are constructive and benevolent for the whole.

If you read many of the works and writings that aim to 'analyse' the whole in order to understand the whole, you will probably find contradictions either within the method, for example scientific method, within the process, for example professed exclusivity within a faith, or with any of the conclusions or exclusions resulting from either of these. They are full of assumptions, or are writings that go beyond the core messages of the avatars that evolved and manifested them. The avatars' messages were intended to be neither exclusive nor conclusive.

Conclusions are one of the foremost contradictions because within eternity and infinity there simply can be no end. As

Ludwig Wittgenstein, one of the most eminent philosophers of modern times showed in his ground breaking work, *Tractatus Logico-Philosophicus*, neither words nor mathematics can *conclude* ultimate understanding or knowledge. Therefore we are all within an on-going *learning* model, a perfect learning model, in which each Being is tested through service to one another. *Exclusion* from the whole is self-evidently a contradiction.

I had the privilege of leading a group of sixty young analysts on a five day course on professional self-development. The basis of the course was how to be authentic, by being one-self and not pretending to be something else to others. The premise is that in doing so you will build trust and relationships, one of the most important things to do in collaborating with others in order to achieve a constructive and benevolent outcome, which is also the basis for leading a *moral* life. Deceiving others is one of the worst things that any Being can perpetrate, but deceiving one-self is by far one of the most self-destructive. Deception can be highly self-deceptive when it starts in one-self.

During this training course, one of the trainers gave an insight into how to achieve service through work. He said there are three broad types of work: having a job, a career or a vocation. The first helps you to survive, and may be necessary at times. The second helps you to progress in your professional learning, but is essentially for you, serving you. The last of these is the equivalent of having a calling, or of serving others.

Some of the more obvious examples of a vocation or calling are nursing, charity projects or faith ministry. However, the principle of vocation can be applied to any type of work, provided that it there is *never* any intention to cause harm to others, *and* the authenticity of your actions support your intention. Integrity creates continuity.

If you have worked in commerce, you will probably have heard the terms 'quality of service' or 'product quality'. The best way of describing this is as being 'fit for purpose'. Since what you produce, the *outcome*, can only be fit for the purpose of those you are producing for or are of service to, nothing that you do will have any quality of value unless it is for others. If you want to be the best you can be, then quality must also be a part of the virtue of excellence if you are also authentic about excelling in what you are trying to do.

You will know when you have found your true vocation or calling when the work that you do gives you the personal joy and the opportunity for personal development and learning *through* that service to others. Therefore it does not really matter if you are a parent, tend communal gardens, serve food or beverages, build commercial systems, are a surgeon, look after family or friends, or whatever else you do in your work, provided that you do that work with love; in other words, in the service of others, by helping others or by sharing the outcome, *and* by *never deliberately hurting others* either directly or indirectly.

It is our striving to survive that makes Human Beings worldly and base. It is also our greed, wanting more than others, that is our debasement. Why? Because focusing on our wants over the needs of others blinds us to bigger and better possibilities, things we have already benefited from through the giving of others around us and before us, in other words the universal concept of the common good.

Is *any* type of love the same as pure love? Two situations will help to illustrate and frame the truth.

The first situation is outlined by this additional question: Should the love for our own children be greater than our love for all created Beings?

The incomplete answer is that parental love is partially based our own selfish desires for 'eternal' survival through our genes. However, that should not be interpreted that the love of our children is unimportant; they are also created Beings. They may also be an anchor, and a reason that we strive to survive, if not in fact then within the laws of nature. Our children may be the only cause for which we would be prepared to die.

This second question completes the situation: What other causes *would* we die for?

If we take the view that other love is just as important, we may be prepared to risk our lives for other Beings. If you doubt this, ask any warrior that has truly bonded with his or her unit. There are many instances of warriors sacrificing their own lives to protect those around them, and also those much further away at home. An ancient example is Leonidas and the other Spartans and allies, who knowingly sacrificed their lives during the Battle of Thermopylae in order to protect and save others who would have suffered had they not done so.

What both distinguishes and unites these two situations is the understanding gained from close proximity, common interest and an acceptance of our own relative unimportance to the whole. Our children and family are a part of us, but so are others. Without others our lives would be much shorter and there could be no continuity.

It is highly self-deceptive to deny that there are those who would risk their lives to protect our children when we would not do the same for theirs. It is also hypocritical; hypocrisy is an ultimate form of both deception and self-deception. To say it was their choice to sacrifice is *immoral*, being neither constructive nor benevolent. The first duty of any parent is to set an example that would create a better world for all our children. It cannot possibly be some children to the exclusion of others, since this would not set a good example to our own children. It is not only a contradiction by the genetic laws of nature; it is also a 'sin' or separation from creation and the whole.

Therefore the real gift we can give our children until they can make their own choices is never to implant our own discrimination, but to lead, live and show by our own example and actions our willingness to give and sacrifice part of our lives to theirs, serving not their worldly wants, but rather their innate need for love, support, belonging and safety that we all have within us. To exclude others is deceptive and denies this reality.

The most important dimension of service to consider for all Human Beings is therefore leadership by example. True leaders are those that *serve* their followers.

The most extreme leadership situation is in the universally unacceptable scenario of conflict and war, the opposing force of connection and love. People will say, 'but how do you stop war?' The answer to this is the most simple imaginable: *Do not start war in the first place.*

The only conceivable justification for war can be to stop *known* and *sustained* destructiveness from dark and antagonistic forces, such as Adolf Hitler and the *ideology* behind it, since it is also *known* that all fires will eventually burn themselves out. However, the only other possible justification, even within these circumstances, is when all other strategies have been exhausted *and leadership failure* has been acknowledged.

All conflict and war is deceptive because it is the failure of all other alternatives, and other alternatives are never exhaustible. With authentic leadership, strategy, foresight, insight *and* the negation of personal power, *all* conflict and war is avoidable. Conflict and war is therefore the pursuit of personal power, insufficient insight or foresight of consequences, for example the reparations *imposed by control* on Germany after the First World War, poor leadership or incorrect strategy.

You might liken Sun Tzu's 'Art of War' to the *Art of Peace*. We should also therefore consider Plato's principle of 'Philosopher Kings' to lead in the spirit of constructiveness and benevolence, *everywhere* in the world and within *all* cultures, nations, organizations, and faith or belief systems. This is the effective end of 'us' and 'them', which starts with an understanding and knowledge of the end of 'you' and 'me'.

To uncover leadership deception, which applies in *any* set of circumstances, there are a series of questions that can be asked as a test before electing or following *anyone*:

1. *Would they sacrifice themselves before others?*
2. *Do they think and act in the interests of all, including those within other assumed groups?*
3. *Do they derive personal power from their position, or do they empower others?*
4. *Do they derive personal benefit from the situation other than that which the followers would want for them?*
5. *How would they create collaborative, constructive and benevolent outcomes?*
6. *Do they contradict themselves?*

7. *Would they step down of their own volition if they transgressed any of the preceding questions?*

Trust is earned through *authenticity*. It is displayed and reinforced through *integrity*. No one in their right mind would elect or follow a leader who said, 'follow me, I am deceptive.'!

Deception is a form of control. It is immoral, because it cannot display the values of constructiveness *and* benevolence. It is false, because it has no sustainable benefit, either to the group or to the individual. It runs counter to both the common good and the longer term interests of the individual. If deception gains a personal benefit, it can only be sustained by power or control over others, which is another form of deception, since all created things are essentially the same thing. Deception will reinforce itself until it becomes out of balance with its' environment and is deconstructed. Leadership deception is therefore unsustainable.

There is another perspective to consider: control without any intention to be immoral is a form of *insecurity*, which is often perceived as a weakness in another. The greatest strength any Human Being can aspire to is through acknowledgement of a personal weakness, including the attempted and unsustainable control of others, something that needs experience in order to turn this weakness into a sustainable learning and strength.

If a Human Being attacks a perceived weakness in another, it discloses more about the immorality or insecurity of the perpetrator than the personality being attacked - who is the one who is *not* trying to deceive themselves or others? Conversely, no Human Being should assume that kindness in another equates to weakness. Many Beings have made that mistake. Kindness shows a wisdom and strength beyond measure. The warriors of the Light are leaders that are stronger than any other, and will always be.

A wise leader will construct guidance that prevents self-harm or harm of the individuals and group being led, whether this is within a community, an organization or a nation. This will include rules not to harm other individuals or groups except *perhaps* in exceptional circumstances in order to stop any immediate threat through self-defence, in which case these leaders would need to step down as failed strategists. Potential self-harm of the group through pre-emptive action or failed leadership is a contradiction, even if the leader is the first to suffer or take the risk. As the leader is also a member of the group, all pre-emptive war and conflict is contradictory and unjustifiable. The truth therefore shows that there are no perhaps.

Religious and other belief systems of the good *never* cause war. Only the power and control wielded by individuals over others, using religion or ideology by deception, can do this. You can never beat deception with deception and stand on higher moral ground. The avatars of faith would be horrified by any form of separation, including any form of deception, self or otherwise, that had the possibility to result in conflict. Not one of them professed war or conflict as the solution. Leaders who claim otherwise should be open to question. True leaders serve their followers. Any leader that claims to be a guru cannot be; *self*-declaration is a contradiction.

Interference with the free will mind of others is part of the deception, and cannot be acceptable in any set of circumstances since this is a form of manipulation and control. We cannot therefore choose or make moral choices for others, including the inverse of implanting our discrimination on others, including children. However, this should not be confused with morally protecting, leading and *influencing* others, which means guiding others *in flow* to help them make their own free will choices and decisions. We should therefore encourage children to become aware of sustainable values as soon as they are able, an intrinsic morality based on constructiveness and benevolence.

Is there any such thing as a good or bad organization?

The culture of an organization always comes from its' leadership. Authentic leaders, those worthy of following, are those who serve their followers, never their own self-interest. The only sustainable organizations are those that meet the needs of those they serve based on sustainable and moral values that make the world a better place for all, both in this world and the next.

*At the end of the day the world does not have to be perfect, just better than when the day started.*

# 7. WHERE DO WE GO?

THE QUESTION 'WHERE DO WE GO?' pre-supposes that there is a 'here' and 'there'. There is no such thing in reality as *here* and *there*, since overall space is a dimension of God or the Universe, the whole or The One, except in *thought* perception. *Here* and *there* are word distinctions to help make sense of the temporal world that we can see and 'measure'. This thought exists to help manage our own energy by looking at the place where a temporary form or object exists through our senses of observation.

Despite this, the distinction *within space* can be used to help identify systems and environments that we can then look at to help understand the nature of each one along with its' 'critical mass', remembering that they are *all connected* at many different levels and therefore only a *part* of the whole. The total sum of understanding can only be partial during temporal life. The Human brain is not large enough to hold *all* knowledge.

As Human Beings, it might be useful to imagine four areas of space dimension: 1) during temporal life (including material life as a Human Being), 2) at temporal death, 3) during purely spiritual life (immateriality), and 4) after purely spiritual life (including service by going back into a temporal rebirth). The four link back or *incarnate* in a cycle of growth. The common essence is spirit, which is continuous and eternal.

Spirit, the energy of Being, connects all four areas of space dimension. Within each Being is the soul or 'seed' that carries the innate learning through the core of its' energy. At the highest level, the purely spiritual, this energy and learning, plus new and additional learning acquired during temporal life, is shared through conscious spirit within *One mind.*

This is analogous to individual neurons (souls) working together through synapses (connections) via electricity or chemicals (energy) within the brain (the universal mind) to create thinking and resulting creative possibilities for the *whole* or One, God's will manifested.

This is not to suggest that God is made up of individual thoughts; it is essentially the other way round. The One 'seeds' by creating souls with free will choice to manifest possibility within firstly the spiritual world and then within the temporal.

The reason I am describing this in the order from the temporal 'up' to the spiritual is that this is probably easier to understand and visualize from the perspective of the temporal world, conceived as the ascension from the temporal to Heaven, or eternal life. However, since the whole is One, it does not matter which way this is looked at as 'direction' is simply a concept to help understand movement and reforming within space. If a Being is at the ninth Gate of Light, it would be seen as nothing more than a pure service to The One or God, a soul or type of 'neuron' within and *of* the whole.

This leads us as to why we come into the temporal world as Beings.

*The purpose of life is to learn and grow,* to help develop, teach and share that learning from our experiences as Beings so that we can become more sustainable and therefore *evolve* spiritually and temporally, serving other Beings with that learning. An example might help explain how that process works.

One of the most difficult lives I can imagine is being a Gladiator in ancient Rome, where as a slave you must kill in a public arena in order to stay alive, merely for public entertainment. You might say, what could possibly be learnt from such an experience and be shared with others that could help them grow? The naive answer would be 'the survival of the fittest'. The enlightened answer would be this: *it is better to have an honourable death with people watching your life, than to have a dishonourable life without anyone noticing it. Everything happens for a reason.* Gladiators were taught to *embrace* pain, suffering and death. Many people had to go through unimaginable pain and suffering to create those learnings.

You could judge that to kill or to risk someone else's life without first risking your own is morally wrong. In this you would be morally correct. Two wrongs can never make a right, but there can be lessons. So which is worse, the Gladiator who believed in being the best they could be in order to stay alive, without any real choice as to how to live, only how to die, or those who sent them to their deaths? What about the animals that were also slaughtered? What about those who *watched* them die, and did not care how *they* suffered?

We can understand and accept that such a culture is morally incorrect and potentially barbaric, yet some would still hunt, kill or make other sentient Beings suffer for entertainment or food, or go to war and create on-going conflict, falsely in the name of religion, or deceptively in the pursuit of personal benefit, power or control. We also know that there are those who would command risking the life of other Human Beings without risking their own lives or being prepared to suffer or die first through or as a result of their decisions as leaders by example. Controlling the lives of others to suffer is the very *worst* form of separation or sin. To deny free will through control or selfish interference is to deny the true nature of creation in conscious Human Beings, and therefore the *ultimate* separation from the common good and The One.

Sometimes we can all be *watchers*; all it takes for the bad to prosper is for the good to do nothing. The lessons can be learnt at many levels.

Using free will choice, the solution to avoiding this in *one-self* is simple: *choose* whether or not to have self-will control of the self, which is the essence of the Divine, leading to the moral choice between *good and bad actions*. This essentially means that during our Being, at whichever level, we must either practice self-control or be impacted by governance from the Creator of free will and potentially lose consciousness. Everlasting life has a price.

What happens when we die a temporal death?

All material things consist of energy that is either conscious or unconscious of existence. Within a Human Being, during temporal life, it is mostly a critical mass of conscious energy, or consciousness, which also observes its' own form as a Human Being, plus the current form of other objects. Borrowed energy that is connected to the Universe can be called spirit energy. Spirit is the energy of action.

During the 20th Century, experiments were carried out on the bodies of Human Beings after they had died, when their brain activity had ceased. Their hands were placed on photo-sensitive plates to see how long after death the energy continued to be absorbed by the plate. The energy of those that had died peacefully did not last for more than few hours. Those who had died violently took much longer; their previously harnessed energy took longer to depart from the temporal body. If you are still sceptical, a psychic who can see the aura of energy around a Human Being can also tell the colours within that aura, which changes based on the feelings within. Those with black auras have dark thoughts or Being. Those with white, gold or purple elements are connected to a higher level. Red denotes some type of anger or extreme discomfort with a situation. Seeing red is literal. This can be proven with special aura cameras that are able to record this phenomenon.

This spirit energy also helps explain why those with a near death experience often report that they have seen a white light or white 'tunnel'. This is simply a spiritual preview of the pure white energy that contains all Light. Some of us call this home. The soul, the energy of Being, will be preserved to carry this consciousness forward *if it is worthy of creation*, in others words that creation is *served*.

What happens once the pure energy of the angelic realm is capable of being reached by the Being just released from a temporal life?

This depends on what has happened during temporal life - the life that has been lived, plus the karma of previous lives. The status of learning is attached to the soul in a quantum of energy.

For those souls that are worthy to return to life again, to continue the learning, the energy is held in space until the next time the Being returns to the temporal world. Some call this process *reincarnation*, another incarnation of the same free will Being that has been seeded. Some believe that we are given the choice as to which learning we want to take on, which learning we are prepared to accept next. Eventually all possible learnings must be manifested within all Beings, with non-separation from others being one of the most important lessons, as it underpins an understanding of all other lessons, that *everything* is connected and a part of the whole, or The One.

When angels (the messengers) return, they return to Source, the learning's are consolidated and new intentions are created by The One. These are formulated into messages for other messengers, who can be born into a temporal form or communicate via *spirit* to guide individuals. Some call this individual and internal guidance the *conscience*. New and additional messages are created based on a cumulative learning, to help, share and guide. Some messages come back into the temporal world through newly created Earth angels, those who have previously passed through the Gates of Light.

Those that have learnt all important lessons are given the choice as to whether to serve within the angelic realm or return as temporal Beings to serve other temporal Beings. Those that are able to teach are also given the choice to do so, for example Shakespeare and Plato. Teaching is one of the best ways of learning the lessons of growth and refining them.

Those Beings that would hurt other Beings are not so fortunate. Their consciousness is carried into 'white noise' until they are released again, into a world that progresses their journey back to the Light. It is impossible to learn in white noise since the mirror is not sufficiently clear to be able to learn. It is much like being conscious, only with a highly fractured mirror all around limiting any reference back to one-self and what is known and can be learnt from connection with others. This is the isolated place of Being. Some call this purgatory, where unworthy souls are purged until the world changes and becomes a more progressive place to learn before their return.

Energy that has been created cannot be destroyed by a God of love, even if a particular energy Being rebels through free will against the Creator. However, the energy can be dispersed, such that consciousness has no critical mass, is *lost* and the energy is re-used as part of the *creative* process. The 'seed' or the soul is effectively removed from universal consciousness, such that it can never cause harm again. This is analogous to removing cancerous cells from the body. The mutant cell, the energy Being that chose to separate through free will, may be redistributed to create benefit for others as a reflective mirror for others to learn from. This is the shadow cast by light to know the direction of the return to Source. Each moment, through each life learning experience, the shadow becomes a lighter shade of gray.

The mirror is, to some extent, within all of us, within all Human Beings. This so that we can learn from each other what can work and is sustainable, and what can never work except in short term existence, by observing how we each want to be and live our lives through reflection. We are all a part of energy that takes different forms during life, in transition and after life.

In transition, from the temporal to the spiritual world, the spirit departs the temporal body releasing most of the spirit energy that has been borrowed during our lives. The innate learning is carried forward within the quantum energy of the soul to be shared and fully connected within the spiritual world with other Beings and the whole. This is the point we can fully understand and *know* that we are part of The One, or God, that is *no thing*. You might ask why all Human Beings cannot have full access to this knowledge and energy within temporal life. The answer is three-fold.

Firstly, all Human Beings can have partial knowledge of the complete symphony and recognition of the divine while hearing music that moves the soul, in feeling and touching the joy of nature, in seeing new life being created, or in experiencing pure and self-less love. We all need to believe in something that is inspirational and stirs the soul. Even if you are still at this moment not convinced of God's existence, a belief in the common good is of no less importance since the process is a stepping stone across the river. Just listen to the words of John Lennon in his famous composition 'Imagine' to understand. A belief in God is of no value unless it is first lived that way.

Now *imagine if* those who would abuse others had full knowledge and were able to use that knowledge and the enabling energy to their own advantage, to administer more abuse within the temporal world. There have been many examples of people who would do so, because they have *chosen* to abuse and exploit their position even with the partial knowledge that they have. They are easy to identify. They are the ones who take power and control over others for their own benefit, as opposed to empowering and supporting the free will choice of others and serving others without contradiction. The truth is that, if you choose to live within the world of the common good, you would want to *imagine* such people never having access to complete knowledge.

Secondly, if Human Beings had full knowledge, each Being would have to remember everything that had been experienced, including the pain of how each lesson had been learnt. Imagine if you were that Gladiator. You would have access to be able to recall and feel again, seeing your friends die and the manner and pain of your own previous suffering and death. It is a trade. In much knowledge there is much sorrow.

Thirdly, the Human brain is not large enough to hold all of this knowledge. It can only be accessed by connection with others, through spiritual energy and Being.

Can all space dimensions be connected from the here and now, within the temporal life, to see and serve the connected whole?

The answer is yes, provided the Being has previously passed through the eighth or ninth Gate of Light. The Gates of Light are described in Chapter 8.

All of this raises the question as to why or how we, Human Beings, plus other Beings in the Universe, were created, where we come from and where we go to. This is difficult to answer, but an imaginary story might help. This story is not to be taken literally. Words are a primary tool to help conscious understanding (in addition to what we feel and know through instinct and observation), but they are limiting and largely definitive. This is because words are discriminatory and *limited* by definition, whereas the One is *everything* and *infinite* and therefore in truth without definition.

Initially, imagine nothing, or *no thing*. Imagine the first awareness, but it is singular, a singularity. Then think: If this was me, this initial singular awareness, could it be more 'interesting'?

One could then decide to have a party, but only The One would be there. So One decides that to have a party, *a part* of One would manifest as something else, the same as One, but acting like a *mirror*, a mirror self. This is still One, but creation has now created two parts, a part of the whole, each a mirror reflection of the other. The cosmic analogy would be observation of the moment of the 'Big Bang', positive and negative energy, matter and anti-matter. The Human analogy would be cell division within the body. The two parts work with each other and for each other. If One destroys the other, then creation is back to square One, which in mathematics would be One!

To have a party would also need a room, a venue if you like, essentially *space* to accommodate One and grow with the emerging possibilities.

Now imagine that it would be better with more of the same One's at the party, further sub-divisions but still a part of the whole or One. Each of the sub-divided parts of the created two-way mirror would have attributes that are *in essence* the same, but at the same time also diverse *in order* to create further 'interest' within and for the party hosted by The One. The chemical analogy would be creation of a simple but unstable element such as hydrogen, then helium which is more stable but inert, then lithium which is a metal and can create physical form, etc.

The 'problem' with this party is that all the elements are essentially the same energy reforming. Imagine being at this party where there was just One consciousness of this. The reforming would be like having non-learning robots at the party. It would be far more 'interesting' if the robots could help the diversity by becoming self-regulated Beings. The Human analogy would be to create twins. These twins have the same Source but different experiences and existence. The Source has free will, because it has created, and the same would therefore be created in its' product. This then sub-divides further, until the party has all its' participating guests, for now. The self-regulated Being is manifested, with an 'interest' in each other.

To do this, free will is created within each part. It is through free will that the choice to be diverse is progressed and expanded, essentially to create all possibility by *Being of service* to the whole. Everything is manifested and anything is possible with this free will choice, including *unlimited growth*.

Now imagine that these free will Beings do not recognize their Creator and host, and want to take over the party. The mere intention is separation from the original intention of creating, which must be love because it is for giving. The party becomes disruptive, things could be destroyed and some of the creation is in danger of being reversed. To stop this there are safeguards, loyal guardians to the Creator or host. They recognize to choose this otherwise everything would cease to exist except The One, and back to square One! We call these angels or messengers (from the Greek *angelos*). They protect the whole and all other created Beings, even from their potentially destructive selves. More importantly, the unworthy have also chosen to disconnect from their higher selves, and so do not have access to this knowledge except by personal learning within the temporal world and re-choosing.

The other safeguards to the party are the Gates of Light, the doors into the room, so that those Beings that wish to return who have previously been thrown out can do so. In addition, newcomers are welcome, provided that that they have passed all the required tests, which are based on the lesson and *learning*. All spirit energy can be recycled, shared and re-used for the common good. The learning is how to make the party sustainable and enable a permanent connection.

There is not a Being that has not separated or sinned, or tried to, even if only within a temporary thought, at some point. With separation, self-destruction becomes possible, consciously manifested so that we can learn from it. Consciousness can be 'disappeared' by removal of its' critical mass if a Being created from that energy is or becomes destructive. Worse, collective separation can result in annihilation, for example destroying our ability to survive on a living planet.

At another level, if a Being consciously chooses to separate, it effectively chooses to separate from the whole of creation. If it is not part of creation, it will be granted its' wish to not to exist. The model is self-regulating and consequently sustainable.

You might ask how an omnipotent Universe can allow this separation in the first place. Firstly, it is a consequence of free will choice. Secondly, we separate in order to understand and learn from the process of reunification. The top-down model now becomes bottom-up, and is self-sustaining provided that the separation is *temporary*. The polarity has become a duality.

The Universe is a quantum of dynamic brought into being. Its' complexity is the evolution of possibility until it finds sustainability, then it becomes self-sustaining. It is its' own first cause. The story is not complete. The story will never be complete because it is infinite and eternal. If the party ends, The One will create a new party, another Universe, perhaps another 'Big Bang'. There can be many parties at the same time.

I hope that this story helps understanding of *where do we go*. The question *'where do we go?'* is now the same as *'where do we come from?'*. The main question then is *'how are we able to return?'*.

*If you are bleeding, look for*
*someone with scars.*
**– Tristan Morell**

# 8. THE GATES OF LIGHT

THE LINK BETWEEN THE GATES of Light and *service* is not always easily understood.

The Gates are like the layers of an onion. The onion grows from the inside out. The more you become part of the skin, the more you realize that you protect the core, much like parents protecting children, or the ability to nurture growing.

The Gates of Light are protective layers or safeguards connecting the path back to Source (or to God, Allah, Jehovah, Heaven or The One). They are passed in stages by those who recognize and acknowledge their own loyalty to the Creator. They also prevent the unworthy causing disruption and destroying the fabric of creation. The learning of the Gates of Light defines the path as to how knowledge of the truth is acquired and accessed, and brought back again into the temporal world.

There are nine Gates of Light in total, seven plus two. The first seven are accessible from the temporal world by all conscious, free will Beings. The last two, the eighth and ninth, are accessed for the first time after temporal death for those who have passed the first seven Gates.

Those Beings that exist in the temporal world that fully accept the Christ Being within them for the first time and live in total service to The One, alongside all other created Beings, can access all nine of the Gates of Light during successive lives. True *Christ*ianity is an acquired knowledge of the Divine, living and learning through the journeys and ways taught by *all* of the avatars, giving *many paths* back to Source. This enables all conscious Beings to serve others to the same level as the Christ Being (the manifest will of God or The One) *within the temporal world*, through *individual* free will choice *within* any chosen faith or belief system. The paths are not *exclusive,* but the Gates of Light are the same for all.

Those who temporarily choose to be in the shadows below the first Gate also have free will, because this initial level of shared consciousness is a mirror in others that enables the help and understanding to choose an *individually* sustainable path for each Being.

The good news is that all Human Beings are capable of progressing, of recognizing the Christ Being within them and living that way, and of ascension back to Source. Human Beings were created in the image or *vision* of God. However, the majority of Human Beings have not yet progressed beyond the first Gate of Light. There are primary conditions or tests to pass before passing through each Gate. I will outline this channelled knowledge and give examples of real Human lives of which you may be familiar or that you could research yourself. Some are famous and some less so.

Before the first Gate is 0, representing both nothing, before the start of the journey, and *no thing* or The One, the duality of God's creation which is both infinite and circular (please see Chapter 5). The first Gate represents recognition of the whole of creation, the single line that points to a joining between Heaven and Earth, and vice versa, the number I.

Although the Gates appear to be one-directional and linear, they are circular in nature, bottom to top then back down to the temporal, and top down from the angelic then back again, as each new learning is created and perfected within the model. There have been other models and there will be more. Did you think that Human Beings were the only Beings created, the first or the last? Or that *the* Big Bang was anything more than *a Big Bang*, incompletely observable through the current laws of physics which can by definition only be a part of the whole? The fifth dimension is a progression in the current learning model.

To pass the first Gate of Light, each Being must not only show that they recognize the nature of creation, but also that they live by it to the very best of their ability, *The Golden Rule* if you prefer. This is when you recognize love as the driving force of creation, when someone or something else is more important than oneself.

This can be done through *any* faith or belief system, *provided* it is done both morally and with integrity, *without any form of separation*. This means that you must make every effort to make your peace with everyone before being able to progress. You cannot use God as a reason or an excuse to harm another Being, Human or otherwise. You must aim for completely the opposite and to *help* others to understand this. Good early examples of this would be Zoroaster, Lao Tse, the Buddha and Marcus Aurelius.

Zoroaster was one of the first Human Beings to teach of the one God (Azura Mazda) who is at the same time cardinal, creation (the *what* that *is* Azura Mazda, also *within* creation and therefore temporal), free will (the choice that was created for Beings) and morality (the collaborative values by which to live). Note especially the duality of the cardinal and the temporal in Zoroaster's message. His message pre-dated that of the Buddha.

Lao Tse taught of the Tao, or the Way. He based this teaching on living in the moment, acceptance of the life you live, and without expectations. In following your heart, you connect with creation and the Way things are meant to be. Everything happens for reason. Only a lack of faith can doubt that this happens.

The Buddha's message was to reinforce and *sustain* this message through the teaching of a *Middle Way* between the extremes of light and dark, existence and learning, or the circumpunct or balance between the cardinal and the temporal, which enables *the connection between Heaven and Earth* and a return to Source (the whole or One).

Marcus Aurelius was a Roman Emperor and philosopher. Within his book, Meditations, which is a philosophy of *service*, you can observe the link to the teachings of Zoroaster and the Buddha. He looked to nature to find lessons in balance and harmony. Using this example of how to live, it seems that even the most powerful people on Earth are capable of learning how to do this and to serve others.

Once the first Gate of Light has been passed, there is no turning back to a lesser life. Any choice to do so would be seen as a betrayal of the pure love that is given. If you do, this is essentially the first time you will unleash Universal displeasure, which Human Beings might interpret as Divine fury, because you have become unworthy of that gift and would have to re-learn that love is for giving (in order to be forgiven again).

Ascending through the first two Gates of Light are the *most important* since, once these two have been passed, the passage from the third to the seventh Gate can accelerate quickly.

The second Gate of Light represents the Chiron, or the wounded healer. All healers have passed the second gate, a gift for service at both higher and lower levels. The *wound* is why most Human Beings have not passed beyond the first Gate.

To do this, you must be prepared to sacrifice your own life for others in the name of the *common good*, knowing and accepting that you may die in service of and for others. This requires extraordinary courage, and consciously thinking and acting despite your fears.

Chiron represents two symbols: Chi (X), the cross-roads, and Rho (P), the key. Chi is the 22nd letter of the Greek alphabet, comprising 2 and 2, the *collaboration* of the temporal warriors of the Light. Ch'i is also the life-force in Chinese culture. This spiritual link between east and west is not a mere 'coincidence' - language is also symbolic (a signpost) of Universal intention, the *Word* of God; how else could the untransformed consciousness within all faith systems, cultures and belief systems understand the *shared* and common messages *in order to transform*? The numbers 2 and 2 also represent 4, the symbolic cross-roads from the fourth dimension to the fifth, the Golden Age.

Rho is the 17th letter of the Greek alphabet, comprising 1 and 7, indicating the primary link from the first Gate of Light through to the seventh. Combined with Chi, including an overlay of the Greek symbols *Ch*i (X) and *R*ho (P), ChiRho is the *Christ*ogram that represents the Christ warrior. No Being can become a Christ Being or a Christ (Light) warrior until they have passed the second Gate of Light, through self-sacrifice or a sacrifice of the self within.

A good example of a Human Being who has passed the second Gate is Claus von Stauffenberg, a warrior who risked his life in an attempt to stop Adolf Hitler, and who paid the ultimate price, including his own torture and death. You might argue that he and the other Valkyries were not successful in this act, but that is not important since it is based on *own* sacrifice for the *common good* not the result itself. 'Greater love has no man than this: that a man lay down his life for his friends.' - John 15:13.

You can see, with hindsight, how the Universe works in what Stauffenberg and the other Valkyries achieved. Had they managed to stop him directly, Hitler would have become a martyr, with a possible extension of the war and even greater and longer term destruction for many innocent Human Beings. As it was, the intention unbalanced to the extent that Hitler was never the same again, and as a result the war he promulgated came to an earlier and ultimately successful conclusion, saving additional Human-created pain and suffering.

There are undoubtedly those who have died, suffered or risked their own lives in war, including both warriors and conscientious objectors, in the service of others. Provided they acted with the right intentions to serve others in the name of the *common good* and with personal integrity, it may be of comfort to know that they have already passed the second Gate of Light. They have already passed the test, and their passage is assured.

The third Gate of Light represents wisdom. Wisdom is *partial* knowledge, the number 3 being an incomplete version of the number 8 or infinity pointing from Heaven to Earth. The number 8 represents the infinite angelic realm, when temporal Beings can depart the temporal world for the purely spiritual world, and vice versa.

To pass the third Gate, you must have a love of *wisdom* and seek the *truth*, not for yourself, but to help the *enlightenment of others*.

This journey is your sacrifice of what you would otherwise want for you. The aim will always be for the *common good*.

Philosophy is a love of wisdom, a search for higher meaning and truth. I have already mentioned Zoroaster and the Buddha, two avatars, and Marcus Aurelius the philosopher. Another good example is Plato.

Plato was the first western philosopher to recognize the 'shadow of the forms', that the Light creates a temporary shadow as a form that can be readily seen. Hindus will recognize this as the 'veil of Maya' or *illusion*. Human Beings can see reality in the current physical form but, by seeing beyond that, the true nature of reality can be understood; in other words, the *Source* or *Light* that manifests it. Plato also supported the idea that the most worthy leaders are those with a love of wisdom, knowledge and truth, essentially serving those who elect or follow them, the so-called 'Philosopher Kings'.

The fourth Gate of Light represents awareness of infinite consciousness, such that the mind *becomes* part of Universal consciousness, helping to connect the temporal with the spiritual. This can be glimpsed or felt though the here and now, an immersion in the connection with nature, and sometimes through meditation. A good example of someone who has passed the fourth Gate would be Eckhart Tolle, a successful German writer on inner transformation and spiritual enlightenment.

The fifth Gate of Light represents a two-way inversion of the second Gate. This is the mid-point when angelic warriors are manifested between *both the temporal and spiritual worlds*. This means that previous light warriors and light workers can *awaken* or be awakened to return to service, and new ones are created *with connection to pure spirit*.

The connection is between pure energy and the form of energy. As a result, Beings at this level are able to see or sense pure energy, such as the auras and intention of other Beings, and sometimes the 'past' or 'future'. To pass the fifth Gate, you must want, submit and agree to serve the Universe. All prophets have passed beyond the fifth Gate.

The sixth Gate of Light represents submission to returning to the temporal world whenever required as a warrior of the Light, the symbol of 6 being a spiralling down from the Heavens, a *grounding* of universal intention. Therefore all Beings that have passed the sixth Gate have agreed to progress to the seventh Gate.

The sixth gate, when you are ready, can also be accessed from the temporal world, striving for the balance between the temporal and spiritual within one-self, uniting the sacred and the profane within you, a walking of the Middle Way, a letting go that is a stepping stone into the purely spiritual world.

The seventh Gate of Light, the last of the temporal access is when channelling of the universal intention takes place. All avatars have passed the seventh Gate, sometimes known as *Seventh Heaven*. This is where the Universal mind is connected to the temporal world, and *new* things can be manifested, including the same or a similar message, which was only possible to be corrupted below the first Gate of Light.

The eighth Gate of Light represents angelic service, Beings created for and in service of the Universe. Beings created with this purpose in mind also *serve other Beings* using their own consciousness and free will. New angels can therefore be created from Human Beings, Earth angels. The Earth is a 'seeding' ground for new souls.

Some of the originally created Beings rebelled against the Creator using their free will choice and fell below the first Gate of Light, and tried to use the counter-point to positive and constructive energy by taking actions that promoted chaos and destruction. Demons were angels that chose a selfish path. Many that fell did not submit to the process of the Gates of Light during the battle of Armageddon and so could not return to Source. This outcome was a test of the learning model as a precursor of the process that Human Beings also have to learn.

In this eighth realm, the intention of separation is no longer possible. To pass the eighth Gate of Light you must agree to the test of true leadership (in Chapter 6).

Beyond the ninth Gate of Light is the structure of the mind of God for the whole, where wholeness or *Holiness* is created. This is where the perfect learning model is conceived, in other words, the Universe is created and where all created *minds, the* thoughts of energy, are connected, and serve and love as One. The symbol 9 represents spiralling *up* to the Heavens, the inverse of 6.

Ten (1 and 0 conjoined) is an infinite circulation or repeat of the model. It is used in binary code, the structure of the Universe, also used in mathematics, another type of *created* language. It is the structure of energy, reality and all forms of creation.

The numbers 1, 2, 3 and 4, representing the four main temporal Gates, also add up to the *perfect* number of 10. This connection was first made by the philosopher Pythagoras, the father of mathematics. Pythagoras created the tetractys, a three-cornered pyramid with four points to illustrate this, and was the first to divine the number 10 as the *Holy* number.

The ancient Egyptians also knew this, creating the four-cornered pyramids at Giza. The fifth, the apex, points to and from Heaven. This apex represents and foretold of the fifth dimension, when the Christ Being manifests on Earth, and the transformation of Human consciousness is accelerated towards Heaven. The timetable was set and channelled during the time of the Mayans, preparation for the Day of Judgement after tribulation.

However, this judgement is not the final one. Human Beings that have not passed the first Gate of Light will reincarnate to have other chances to pass these Gates using only their free will to choose until the current experiment is completed in 2,536 A.D., the Last Judgement.

Only *creation* is sustainable during the period of the fifth dimension, the Golden Age, and all creation *is* possible with the Universal intention of love. Who goes to Heaven is written in The Book of Life.

*All things are known within their time.*

# 9. INTENTION

THIS BOOK TOOK APPROXIMATELY FIVE weeks to write, and another few weeks to refine. The Book of Life took five weeks from beginning to end. Some of the philosophy within them, the understanding, was penned many years before. Sometimes I set my alarm to awake at 4am, the best time to get help. This shows the power of 'receiving' and being connected at many different levels through personal sacrifice and acceptance. Giving is receiving.

Many messages were given during that time, some directly and others through an intuition that helped to connect all this information and enable it to *flow*. In all cases I had to understand through both direct and indirect experience and acceptance of the knowledge *within me*. It is as though I *already* knew. Time had no meaning, except to manage the energy and enable my mind, body and soul to cope with the knowledge and changes within. This was Universal intention. It is as though I was surrendering and my energy was being directed. All you have to do is go with the flow, the *influence* or intuition, my conscience. God is my conscience. I know that I belong to and serve The One because of this process.

In both books, the chapter headings were written down in order and without change. When this happened, I received confirmation by a *quickening*, something that feels like an energy surge going through your body. I was also told five months beforehand by Tristan Morell, a highly enlightened Human Being and one with whom I have a deep soul connection, that on 17^th August 2010 that I would make a serious commitment to someone. That was the date I finished typing The Book of Life. I now know that this commitment was to The One. I still had to make choices when the door was opened. I am and will always be amazed at the power of creation.

Intention is when you intend something. It starts within your thoughts and then manifests through your actions. I am not sure, knowing now what I had to go through, that I would have chosen and gone through that journey in order to be able to write this. At times it was painful in the extreme, but I coped, I carried on and it was meant to be. That process of surrender gave me the guidance and information to experience what I had to and to be able to write it down and share it with others.

I travelled to places that I *knew* I had to go to, including Auschwitz-Birkenau, where around one million Human Beings were exterminated. At the end of each emotionally and spiritually exhausting day there, something extra-ordinary happened: a flock of birds flew over each of the two concentration camps, something that did not usually happen according to previous visitors I had spoken to. God works in mysterious ways. That is how you and I get the inspiration and sometimes the confirmation of what we are doing.

During a particularly difficult period, I asked my dear friend and colleague, one with his own deep scars, why I was not getting any help, guidance or sign. I felt that I was in trouble, not able to cope. He replied by telling me a story.

Once there was a man who had fallen overboard at sea and was at risk of drowning. Along came a boat and someone offered to throw him a life-line. He declined saying that he was waiting for help from God. This happened a second time with another boat, and again he declined. The third time it happened he got it and understood, and so did I.

My friend and the story *were* my life-line. I had learned. This story was handed down to him by his own healer and teacher, further evidence of intention, connection and continuity, both through 'time' and through heart-warming soul connections.

Anything is possible. Intention, when it is created, becomes part of the Universe, which is created in the here and now. As the saying goes 'there is no time like the present'. It is created through both our thoughts and actions.

We can choose to believe in God or not. If we choose not to believe in good then we are in dangerous territory and missing the point at every level. Human Beings cannot survive without Godliness, goodness or benevolence, the gift of creation.

We are here to learn, and the best way of learning is by living and experiencing both the good and the bad. We can only learn from our mistakes, or choose not to (which seems like a particularly stupid thing to do). Yet it has taken me many times before I sometimes learned the lesson, mainly because my ego didn't want to let go or the lesson was too painful. I had to learn to reconnect and swallow my pride, forever questioning why I was doing this when the process hurt so much.

There is a duality in all of this.

There is a saying that 'there can be no light without dark'. If you reflect on this, it is a paradox. You will come to recognize and understand that this also means that 'there can be no dark within light'. So, good intention, for all of us and *by all of us*, would be that 'darkness is nothing more than shadow cast by the light'.

This *is* the way back to truth, the path to enlightenment. This realization was a major learning for me.

When I came to also realize that I had signed up to this long before I can remember, I finally understood the connection between the past, present and future that began in this life when I was six years old. At that age I had glimpsed infinity and eternity. It is difficult to describe, except that it is something like *time standing still* within the moment, except that the moment lasts a little longer than expected.

This was better described by a friend who had asked if I had experienced that no-thing-ness, when time or change ceases to be. She said that she had felt that only once, when she had held her new born son for the very first time. I remembered that I had felt that also at the moment when I witnessed each of my children being born. I wanted to be no-where else, in no other place, in no other time, this *was* the moment and always will be. Maybe at that moment both she and I had witnessed the miracle of creation, the seeding of a soul, a purer possibility.

Was there a continuity of service in these observations? I undoubtedly think that this happens at many levels. I received confirmation of this during my own process of learning, which has been throughout my life since I was that young child, emotionally, intellectually, physically and spiritually.

This six year old child's experience of connection manifested many years ago on a family holiday in the south of England. I was playing on a children's climbing frame, on my own, and looked up at the sky. The gray clouds billowed in the wind, and it was then that I saw or felt it, that connection with the eternal.

Forty-five years later, I went on a salsa dancing holiday in the same area of England. I decided that I would find the exact place that this six year old had remembered. The buildings had changed, but the large open space was still there, without the climbing frame which had probably long since gone.

I was thinking about where it had happened, the exact spot, and was looking at a patch of ground but wasn't entirely sure that this was it. Just before this happened, I noticed a large bird of prey take off in the distance to my right. While contemplating the original place, the bird swooped very low over the exact location I was looking at. This was my confirmation. I then stood again in exactly the same place as I had forty-five years earlier. The quickening happened again.

I have a big personal ambition before I die: to dance like a Cuban, like a purely connected spirit in flow with the meaning and the essence of the music. During another dancing weekend, I attended a class on the *Orishas*, spiritual dances that come originally from Africa. The African slaves that were transported to the Caribbean were banned from performing these dances, and so they perfected something called the Rumba, a side to side stepping in the line of ankle chains in unison, as One. This later evolved into another dance called the Son. The Son then progressed into Salsa, interpreting the different rhythms and flavours within the salsa music, itself a mixture and progression of different types of music. Salsa is Spanish for 'sauce'. Maybe God is the *sauce* (or Source) in all of us, the original connection within us, and the spirit of the Orishas! Maybe all religious faiths could make the same connection with each other.

I could tell many stories that have happened in a very short space of time during this journey, too remarkable to have been coincidence. I will restrict it to a few to give some idea of the serendipity that is in play, a design if you will that is difficult to fathom, and impossible to anticipate.

One of particular note is that I had never seen an eagle flying outside of a zoo and in the wilds of nature before the age of fifty. Then, during the space of two months, in two different countries while travelling for The One Project, I observed six different eagles flying very close by. Suffice to say that I took these as signs that I needed to overcome my own unwillingness to carry on and continue with the journey.

During the summer of 2010 I travelled over 3,000 kilometres in eleven days, driving from England through France, Switzerland and Italy, and back again. I risked my life on that journey, something I will not expand upon so as not to upset my mother if she read this!

During this time, three extra-ordinary experiences out of many are worth recalling as they happened. Each was totally unexpected. I had not booked any hotels, since I was not fully aware of the actual route that I must take until I was on the road each day. I was living in the moment, in the flow of *service* and *learning*.

The first experience was when driving south through country roads in France, and I ignored the satellite navigation system that persisted in instructing me to turn left. Instead I turned right, following my instincts, guidance or flow. I came upon a very straight and long road, an ancient Roman road. I *knew* that I had been there before through the *quickening*, only that time I had been walking and riding a horse (obviously not at the same time). Yet I had not visited this route before, at least not is this lifetime. I then ignored the navigation system again, and found another long, straight road that bisected the first road at right-angles. I knew where I was. This was the site of the Roman fort, the main command post before the Battle of Alesia with Vercingetorix and the Gallic tribes in 52 B.C. This was a recall of an incarnation, and a connected awareness accompanied by another quickening, a link to the past and to a very different life with very different values.

The second extra-ordinary experience was on the same trip, again when I had had ignored the car's navigation system and followed my guide or instincts. I ended up on the outskirts of a town called Salsomaggiore Terme, a place I did not know. I kept on driving until I *knew* where I had to be. This was when I had parked my car in a road facing the church of Saint Anthony.

As I walked up to the church and down the left hand side, I saw a group of young children playing, supervised by a beautiful young Italian woman. Music was coming from a portable music player. She looked at me, directly in the eyes, and immediately changed the music. The song that she played was Mrs. Robinson. The words came on, *'And here's to you, Mrs. Robinson, Jesus loves you more than you will know. God bless you, please Mrs. Robinson. Heaven holds a place for those who pray'.* The lyrics stopped me in my tracks. I immediately turned and walked back through the doors into the church.

On the left of the church facing the altar was a beautiful painting of a warrior hanging on the wall. He was kneeling, praying for and accepting absolution. I sat and prayed for forgiveness, for past transgressions. It was a very emotional experience, and another quickening.

The third experience that I will recount is equally unusual. I continued on the journey to Rome via other places and, whether by chance or design, I entered the city through what I noticed was the Porta Maggiore. The name link with Salsomaggiore was not lost on me. I drove the car through the intimidating Roman traffic, miraculously without an incident, and drove straight into a parking space, the only one available. This was free to park in all day, in the centre of Rome, opposite the Column of Marcus Aurelius, very near to where I needed to be. I was there to go to the Coliseum, another place of death, and the main arena of the Gladiators, and St. Peter's Square in Vatican City. The energy at the Coliseum was massively and sadly overwhelming, which I felt the closer I walked. All of these connections are connected.

The return journey from Rome took me through Switzerland. It was there that my own passage through the Gates of Light took place. It had lasted about ten minutes. I had passed the test that was set.

During this time, while I was still driving, I could see the world as I could not recall seeing it before. I saw the mountains, beyond the mountains, the road ahead, and the surface of my eyes at the same time. Others will know this as four-dimensional viewing. Time stood still again. Many will not have experienced this, until their time comes and when their transformation accelerates, then they will know what to expect and to have no fear.

This road trip, covering many miles in eleven days, gave the intense experience that is now recorded in the first book of The One Project: *The Book of Life*. In order to write, I had to experience the journey, consciously think about each learning, creating a succinct way of describing them and then acting on this journey by writing it down to help others.

This raises an important question: Which is more important, conscious thought or action? The truth is that they are meaningless without one another.

If we act without conscious thinking, we are simply reacting to the environment, the same as any 'unthinking' organism moving towards self-serving benefit. If we think without action, we cannot prove one way or the other that our intentions are correct. If the intention is for sustainability, a correct way of living and Being, it is part of a learning process that manifests holistic connection and the resulting transformation of Human consciousness.

The outcome of this transformation is that all Human Beings will ultimately choose, consciously, to understand that *Being is based on love*, the same Being that is within you that *also ultimately serves you*. It is the true way to reconnect, sustain and return to Source, because love is the ultimate gift that created *everything* from *no thing* in the first place. This is the true intention of all faith systems.

My own breakdowns and breakthroughs happened frequently throughout this journey, sometimes more than once each day and sometimes continuously over many days. During the past two years there has never been more than three days without a lesson and an important learning, so many that I lost count of them.

The lessons to learn were primarily about my own Being, my understanding, the knowledge I had acquired, my hopes for a better world and the falsity of my fears. More importantly, the process also helped an important understanding of others with their own hopes and aspirations, including learning to live with compassion, never to judge, and always to forgive, but never to forget what is needed to be learnt. Most of the experience and lessons were painful, but all of them were enlightening and ultimately gave me the strength to face and cope with anything and any situation. I broke through the barriers of my own mind. That is why it now relatively easy to make all those connections and record them in a short space of time.

*Stephen Ridley*

As I write this down, the process is cathartic, and the intention is becoming self-fulfilling. Look at the words in this book and you will probably see what this means to me and for the rest of my life. The journey will never end, and I will always agree to serve, but perhaps a better way of putting it is that service is its' own reward when the words become one-fulfilling for all of us. Seen another way, if we all share and return the gift to each other, and help each other to progress through the Gates of Light, ultimately we *serve* each other, and therefore The One.

Do I have an intention that I think would help create collaborative, constructive and benevolent outcomes for all living things?

I think it is captured in these words, written many years before I fully understood them:

> *If we only could*
> *Live as we should,*
> *In God's own loving way;*
> *Neither wrong nor right,*
> *Neither black nor white,*
> *Just differing shades of gray.*

Love all, connect with all, and forgive all. Progress through the Gates of Light, serve One and another, and you will *know*, much more than I now know, long after this life of mine.

Love and peace be with you, and within you, the ultimate intention of the Universe, The One.

*Love takes off masks that we fear we cannot live without and know we cannot live within.*
**- James Arthur Baldwin**